Quantitative R
Methods for Li

Quantitative Research Methods for Linguists provides an accessible introduction to research methods for undergraduates undertaking research for the first time. Employing a task-based approach, the authors demonstrate key methods through a series of worked examples, allowing students to take a learn-by-doing approach and making quantitative methods less daunting for the novice researcher.

Key features include:

- Chapters framed around real research questions, walking the student step-by-step through the various methods;
- Guidance on how to design your own research project;
- Basic questions and answers that every new researcher needs to know;
- A comprehensive glossary that makes the most technical of terms clear to readers;

Quantitative Research Methods for Linguists is essential reading for all students undertaking degrees in linguistics and English language studies.

Tim Grant is Professor in Forensic Linguistics at Aston University, UK.

Urszula Clark is Professor of English Language and Linguistics at Aston University, UK.

Gertrud Reershemius is Professor in Language Contact and Linguistics at Aston University, UK.

David Pollard is Learning and Teaching Support Manager at Aston University, UK.

Sarah Hayes is Senior Lecturer in Technology Enhanced and Flexible Learning at Aston University, UK.

Garry Plappert is a Teaching Fellow in the Department of English Language and Applied Linguistics at Birmingham University, UK.

Quantitative Research Methods for Linguists

A Questions and Answers Approach for Students

Tim Grant, Urszula Clark,
Gertrud Reershemius, David Pollard,
Sarah Hayes and Garry Plappert

Routledge
Taylor & Francis Group

LONDON AND NEW YORK

First published 2017
by Routledge
2 Park Square, Milton Park, Abingdon, Oxon OX14 4RN

and by Routledge
711 Third Avenue, New York, NY 10017

Routledge is an imprint of the Taylor & Francis Group, an informa business

British Library Cataloguing-in-Publication Data
A catalogue record for this book is available from the British Library

Library of Congress Cataloging-in-Publication Data
A catalog record for this book has been requested

ISBN: 978-0-415-73631-2 (hbk)
ISBN: 978-0-415-73632-9 (pbk)
ISBN: 978-1-315-18170-7 (ebk)

Typeset in Optima
by Apex CoVantage, LLC
Printed and bound by CPI Group (UK) Ltd, Croydon, CR0 4YY

Contents

Preface

This book arises out of an Economic and Social Research Council funded research project we have run for our own undergraduate students of English language and linguistics at Aston University in Birmingham, UK. Through the project we examined the attitudes of our students to quantitative research methods and the barriers such students experience in responding to quantitative methods both in their reading of linguistic research and also in the design of their own investigations and studies. UK undergraduate linguistics students have typically given up maths in school earlier than many of their international contemporaries and often come to a university language or linguistics degree programme with negative experiences of working numerically – and yet quantitative methods will always be an essential tool in the linguist's investigative tool box.

Through our research project we developed and evaluated a problem-based learning approach to quantitative methods, which places linguistic questions at the centre. We've learnt to teach quantitative methods little and often in small pieces within nearly every linguistics course/module. We avoid corralling quantitative methods into a separate module and absolutely do not teach quantitative methods in a computer lab or through specialist statistical software. It is our view that twenty-first century students are expert computer users and well able to figure out how software works if they know what they want it to do.

This book is structured into two parts. The first section is a general introduction to statistical ideas. The second, question-and-answer section is the core of this text. Finally, there is also a glossary of terms.

How to use this book if you are a student

If you are a student we suggest that you first read through Part 1 (Chapters 1 and 2). These chapters are intended to help you get your bearings in the terrain of statistical methods. Don't worry about memorising details or content – focus on thinking about the ideas and the logic of what is described. You might come back to this section as a kind of reference. A further reference section is provided by the glossary at the end of the book. This is there to help you look up statistical concepts and ideas when you are reading other parts of the book, or, more importantly, when you are reading research papers in linguistics which use quantitative methods.

The core of this book is in Part 2 – the question-and-answer section. There is some progression through the questions and answers, and you might choose to read this section from beginning to end, but each question is also meant to be read as a standalone section. When you are considering your own research project we hope you will be able to leaf through these questions and answers and find a problem which is a bit like the one you are considering. Matching the structure of your own research problem to the structure of these questions and answers will then enable you to follow the research, data exploration and statistical testing approach associated with that question. In this way we hope to help you learn about quantitative methods through asking your own questions about language and how it is used across contexts.

How to use this book if you are an instructor

If you are tasked with teaching quantitative research methods in a linguistics programme we would further suggest that you start by having conversations with your colleagues. You might even encourage them to look at this book. If you are committed to teaching research methods separately from content modules in linguistics, perhaps have your colleagues suggest questions and provide data for you and your students. Encourage your colleagues to touch on quantitative papers and methods in their own modules, and also encourage them to allow their students to use appropriate quantitative methods across the syllabus. If students are to gain an understanding of the power and pitfalls of using quantitative methods it is crucial that these methods are presented to them as a way of asking interesting questions about language.

Acknowledgements

We are extremely grateful to the Economic and Social Research Council for the award of a grant under its Quantitative Methods: Curriculum Innovation scheme, upon which this book is based. We are also grateful to the students following undergraduate programmes in English Language and Modern Languages at Aston University, who trialled the materials included in this book. We are especially grateful to our colleague Jack Grieve and to the anonymous referee for their input, which was invaluable. Last but least, we wish to thank Nadia Seemungal and Helen Tredget for their forbearance and patience.

Basic statistical ideas

Basic concepts of quantification and number

This chapter and the following one in the first part of this book introduce you to basic concepts in quantitative research. Undertaking quantitative research involves working with numbers and statistics. Statistics involves collecting and analysing numerical data in large quantities drawn from representative samples and from which conclusions or inferences can be made. As a student of applied linguistics, English language or linguistics, you may not have worked with either numbers or statistics very much, if at all, as part of your post sixteen study. Often, statistics can be perceived as too difficult. Why is it necessary, then, to work with numbers and statistics? It is because statistical analysis can be an important tool in linguistic investigation. Many of the research questions we pursue in linguistic research involve measuring and observing data. Examples of this kind of research are to be found in Part 2 of the book.

An important part of learning to use statistics is knowing how to select and how to use the appropriate or right statistical technique as part of a research investigation. Many books in statistical and quantitative methods concentrate on this aspect, explaining the various statistical tests that are available for use. However, in order to understand how statistical tests work, it is necessary first of all to understand the basic and underlying concepts upon which statistical tests depend, and an understanding of these basic concepts is often assumed in many books that deal with quantitative methods. This book is organised differently. The chapters in the first part of this book start by explaining the various concepts that underpin the use of statistics and statistical tests, before going on to explain the tests themselves in the second part of the book. A glossary at the end of the book explains the terms used throughout the book.

This chapter focuses upon **quantification** and **number.** After an initial discussion of quantification, the chapter explains different types of numbers and ways of classifying numbers, including explanations of:

- Nominal numbers (numbers used as names)

- Continuous numbers (numbers you can perform mathematics and statistics on)

- Ordinal numbers (numbers indicating a ranked order)

1.1 Why quantify?

Designing research that concerns the use of quantitative research methods and statistics involves collecting data that can be measured in a numerical way. In order for this to happen, the data set you collect needs to be sufficiently large so that it can be quantified and analysed by drawing upon a range of statistical methods. The word *quantify* derives from the Latin verb *quantificare* and the corresponding noun *quantus*, meaning 'how much' or 'how many'. When we talk about quantifying something, we generally mean that we are going to calculate or measure something and express the calculation or measurement as a number. Quantifying also implies quantity: that is, that the data we measure will be of a size to generate meaningful results. Asking how much data is enough to undertake statistical analysis is a bit like asking how long a piece of string is. It all depends upon the research question you want to answer, or the hypothesis you want to test, as the research questions in Part 2 of the book demonstrate. So, too, is the question of which statistical test to choose to analyse your data. It all depends upon the nature and type of the data you collect and the questions you are asking.

The reason we might want to quantify something will generally be to do with a research question to which we want to find an answer, or a hypothesis we want to either support or disprove. The 'something' we wish to quantify can take many different forms and be of different kinds. The research undertaken in applied linguistics and linguistics research is very similar to that undertaken in other social science subjects such as economics, politics and sociology, in that it is concerned with aspects of human behaviour in areas such as language teaching, phonetics and phonology, sociolinguistics and psycholinguistics. For example, we might wish to evaluate the impact of a new pedagogic approach in language teaching upon students' language learning and its assessment, or provide descriptions of sociolinguistic phonological variation between dialect groups or the rate at which children acquire particular aspects of speech. Linguistics researchers also, in contrast to other social science researchers, undertake textual analysis that relies upon a different set of measures and techniques than those normally used in the social sciences and areas of linguistic research mentioned above. In corpus linguistics and forensic linguistics in particular, textual analysis often concentrates upon the distributional structure of word use, frequency of word use or collocations, or the distribution of errors in language learners' written texts.

Quantifying often involves comparison. Quantifying allows us to make comparisons between, for example, individuals or groups according to some aspect of human behaviour, including the language used. So we can compare our age, weight and height against that of other people, or the number of times men interrupt a conversation as opposed to women. In turn, this allows us to formulate research questions in relation to comparisons between the different categories of data we collect or to test hypotheses about what we might expect to find. To do this the data that is collected can be analysed using an appropriate statistical test. Deciding upon the kind of statistical test you are going to apply to your data depends very much upon the nature of your data, as Chapter 2 of Part 1 explains in more detail.

Aliaga and Gunderson (2002: 14) describe what we mean by quantitative research as 'explaining phenomena by collecting numerical data that are analysed using mathematically based methods (in particular statistics)'. Explaining phenomena is a key element of all research. When we set out to do research, we are always looking to explain something. In linguistics, this could be questions like those given in Part 2 of this book: exploring who actually uses a regional dialect (Low German) and in what way or whether Birmingham English really is more nasal than the varieties that surround it. In quantitative research, we collect numerical data, which is then analysed using mathematically based methods. Quantitative research is essentially about collecting numerical data to explain a particular phenomenon, and particular questions seem immediately suited to being answered using quantitative methods, such as those given above.

The last part of Aliaga and Gunderson's definition refers to the use of mathematically based methods, in particular statistics, to analyse the data. Using statistics to analyse data is the element that puts a lot of people off doing quantitative research in linguistics, as the mathematics underlying the methods appears complicated and frightening. However, as researchers, we do not have to be particularly expert in the mathematics underlying the methods. Much of the statistical analysis we need to undertake in linguistics can be done through the use of computer software, such as a spreadsheet programme like Microsoft Excel, that allows us to do the analyses quickly and (relatively) easily. We do need, however, to understand which statistical tests to apply to our respective data sets in order to answer our research questions, and to do this we need to understand what they are doing.

Statistical analysis normally involves measuring or calculating something that involves the use of numbers. Numbers, though, can be categorised in different ways. For example, we know the date we were born and how old we are, expressed in numbers of years and months. We are all also generally aware of how much we weigh, expressed in pounds, stones or kilograms, and of how tall we are, expressed in feet and inches or metres and centimetres. At its most basic, quantifying is what you do when you express observations as numbers. What, though, is a number? Understanding the concept of number and the different ways numbers can be classified is fundamental to undertaking quantitative analysis. Arguably, it is more important than understanding the formulae employed by different statistical tests, since computer programs do the analysis for you.

1.2 What is a number?

The notion of numbers and counting dates back to prehistory, and most communities or societies, however simple, have some system of counting. As societies and humankind evolved and tribes and groups formed, it became important to be able to know how many members were in any one group, and also how many there were in any other, including possibly the enemy's camp. It was also important to know how many animals there were in a flock or herd and whether or not it was increasing or decreasing in size. 'Just how many do we have' is a question we can imagine members of a community asking themselves or each other, in relation to the tribe itself and any animals they possessed.

It is thought that one of the earliest methods of counting items such as animals or people was with counting or tally sticks. These are objects used to track the numbers of items to be counted. With this method, each 'stick' (or pebble, or whatever counting device was being used) represents one animal or object. This method uses the idea of **one to one correspondence**. In a one to one correspondence, items that are being counted are uniquely linked with some counting tool.

In the picture below, you see each stick corresponding to one horse. If you wanted to 'count off' your animals to make sure they were all present, you could do this by mentally (or methodically) assigning each stick to one animal and continuing to do so until you were satisfied that all were accounted for.

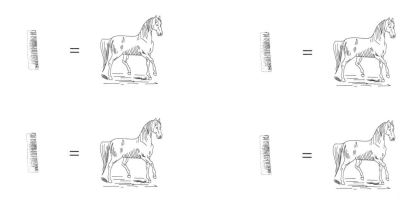

The earliest counting device was the human hand and its fingers, capable of counting up to ten things (although toes were also used to count in certain cultures). Then, as even larger quantities (greater than ten fingers and ten toes could represent) were counted, various natural items like pebbles, sea-shells and twigs were used to help keep count. Another possible way of employing the tally stick counting method was by making marks or cutting notches into pieces of wood, as shown below. Such marks and sticks acted as a counting board.

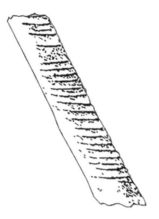

With the invention of writing, symbols were found to represent the numbers just as they were found to represent letters. Over many centuries, the sticks were replaced with abstract objects and symbols. In particular, the top stick is replaced with our symbol '1', the second stick by a '2' and the third stick by the symbol '3'. Different methods of representing numerical symbols were invented, but the most common one was the division in groups of ten.

Another important tool for the use of counting is the **abacus**. An abacus is a manual aid to calculating that consists of beads or discs that can be moved up and down on a series of sticks or strings within a usually wooden frame. The abacus itself doesn't calculate; it's simply a device for helping a human being to calculate by remembering what has

been counted. The modern Chinese abacus, which is still widely used in China and other countries, dates from about 1200 A.D. It is possible that abacuses derive from the earlier counting boards. An Aztec version of an abacus, for example, from circa 900–1000 A.D., was made of maize (corn) threaded through strings mounted in a wooden frame.

The abacus is still in use today by shopkeepers in Asia and Chinatowns in North America. The abacus is still taught in Asian schools and a few schools in the West. Blind children are taught to use the abacus where their sighted counterparts would be taught to use paper and pencil to perform calculations.

There are many different ways in which we can express numbers, depending upon what it is we are counting, labelling or measuring. In this way numbers act as a **semiotic system** in much the same way as language (Ernest 2006). Semiotics is concerned with the study of signs, encompassing all aspects of human sign making, reading and interpretation, across the multiple contexts of sign usage. In this way it can be useful to linguists to think of mathematics as another language for describing the world and acting in it. Maths is just an alternative semiotic system. A semiotic system comprises three necessary components. First, there is a set of signs, each of which can be uttered, spoken, written, drawn or encoded electronically. Second, there is a set of rules of sign production, for producing or uttering single (atomic) and compound (molecular) signs. These rules concern much more than the definition and determinants of a well-formed, grammatically accurate sign. They also concern the sequencing of signs in conversation, such as what sign utterances may legitimately follow on from prior signs in given social contexts. In language the semiotic system centres around or is construed through the linguistic symbolism of sounds and letters that combine into words, utterances, phrases, clauses and stretches of text. In mathematics the system is construed through the use of the mathematical symbolism of numbers and visual display in the form of graphs and diagrams.

Third, there is a set of relationships between the signs and their meanings embodied in an underlying meaning structure. Ernest (2006: 97) suggests that mathematical activity understood semiotically involves the comprehension and production of mathematical signs with the following properties:

1. The basic signs and symbols are drawn from a limited 'alphabet' but are combined to make a large number of compound signs.

2. The production of signs (always in conversation, be it 'live', imagined or otherwise attenuated) involves the production of sequences,

including linear, multi-dimensional and juxtaposed or superimposed sequences of signs.

3. Rules and constraints limit the introduction of signs at each stage in such sequences. That is, they determine which are legitimate and are accepted as such in the conversation.

4. Despite these constraints, which can be much tighter in formal mathematical semiotic systems than in spoken and written language use, there is always an element of creativity in the production of such sequences.

5. Supporting the sign use is a meaning structure that underpins the rules of sign production in terms of preserving key aspects of meaning.

Semiotics and sign systems

• Semiotics is the study of signs and symbols and their use or interpretation. It is concerned with all systems of communication, whether they are verbal or visual.

• Semiotics investigates how meaning is created and communicated. Its origins lie in the academic study of how signs and symbols (visual and linguistic) create meaning. It is a way of seeing the world, and of understanding how the landscape and culture in which we live have an impact on all of us unconsciously. Viewing and interpreting (or decoding) signs enables us to navigate the landscape of our streets and society.

• We are all semioticians, because we are constantly unconsciously interpreting the meaning of signs that surround us – from traffic lights and traffic signs to the colours of flags, the shapes of cars and their number plates, pub and shop signs, the architecture of buildings, and the design of cereal packaging.

• In relation to mathematics, signs relate to the symbolism afforded to numbers and different types of numbers. Like letters, numbers act as a kind of semiotic code.

Systems of measuring things are based on social communities. For example the currency we use in the USA, Canada, Australia and Europe is based upon 100 cents to a dollar or a Euro. In the UK we used to have a system of twelve pennies to a shilling and twenty shillings to a pound. We also had something called a guinea, which was 21 shillings. However, that all changed in 1972 when UK currency moved from shillings to pence, with 100 pence to one pound. The concept of the guinea also disappeared from all walks of life except in relation to the buying and selling of horses in the UK, which still occurs in guineas. Another attempt at changing the UK's system of measurement occurred during the 1980s when measurement of food items changed from pounds and ounces to kilograms, and that of liquids from fluid ounces and pints to centilitres and litres. Such was the public opposition to this move that shops will sell loose goods (such as meat, fruit and vegetables) according to either set of measurements, and pubs still sell beer as pints and half pints. The very fact that currency systems and systems of measurement can be changed in this way shows the semiotic nature of the relationship between numbers and what they represent.

1.3 Classifying numbers

At the most basic level we need to be aware that when we use the word *number* we can mean one of several things and that these must not be muddled up or confused when we carry out quantitative research. A very useful way of looking at this issue is to understand that there are three different categories of numbers (often called variables): *nominal* (sometimes called discrete), *continuous* and *ordinal*. Each of these can play a role in describing linguistic data, and the first step in using them is to have a clear understanding of their differences.

1.3.1 What is a number? Nominal

The word *nominal* relates to *naming* and refers to a use we make of numbers which, when we stop to think about it, we can see has very little to do with numbers at all. Very often we use numbers to name or label things, but we are not counting or measuring them in any way. Consider the way in which we use numbers to name buses. Take the number 63 bus, for example. It is not slightly more than the number 62 bus or slightly less than the number 64 bus. The number 9 bus is not nine-times-anything compared to the number 1 bus. The number 2 bus plus the number 8 bus does not in any sense equal the number 10 bus! This is just not how this type of number works. The numbers on shirts in sports teams are also nominal. In football, for example, the number 1 shirt indicates a particular position on the field (the goalkeeper), effectively naming that player. It becomes possible to recognise a player on the pitch just by their number (such as the footballer Steven Gerrard's number 8 or David Beckham's number 23), and these are functioning as another name for the player. The football player Cristiano Ronaldo has even gone further than this and begun to call himself 'CR7' – explicitly bringing a number into his name – but this has nothing to do with counting, measuring or comparing.

Examples of nominal numbers include:

- Bus numbers
- The number on a sports shirt
- A telephone number
- Road numbers

1.3.2 *What is a number? Continuous*

The second type of number to be aware of is *continuous*. This is the type of number that is used when we are counting or measuring. It is called *continuous* because when using them we can measure at any point on a continuous scale. For example, if we measure the length of something, the value we discover can be any point within the range that we are using, from, for example, 1 centimetre to 10 metres. Thus, your height or weight can be measured and given a numerical value on a continuous scale. The distinction between continuous and nominal numbers can be understood thus: the number of a bus is nominal – say the number 5 from the station to the university – but the number of people on the bus is continuous, varying from none up to about 50 or whatever is the maximum capacity of the bus.

Examples of continuous numbers include:

- The number of people on a bus
- The number of words in a text
- Someone's height or weight
- The number of times that someone speaks in a conversation

The continuous category can be subdivided into two:

1. Continuous numbers that represent *measurement* by a scale of some sort, where the numbers have even gaps between points on a scale (such as a temperature scale of Fahrenheit or Celsius) but for which there is no obvious zero point. This is sometimes called *interval data*.

2. Continuous use of numbers where again the numbers have even gaps between points on a scale but this time with a true zero point, for example a count of the number of words in an essay, the number of people on a bus, or a person's height measured in feet and inches or metres and centimetres. This is sometimes called *ratio data*.

One difference between interval and ratio data is that you can perform multiplication and division with ratio data but not interval data. It makes little sense to say that 32°C is twice as hot as 16°C, but it does make sense to say that a 4000 word essay is twice the length of a 2000 word essay.

1.3.3 *What is a number? Ordinal*

The ordinal category is used to show rank order – for example, the top 40 tracks bought on iTunes or the top ten nightclubs in Ibiza. Ordinal numbers, as the name suggests, are used to put things into an *order*. They are used to *rank* items in a *set* from first to last. Ordinal numbers can be used in a research project when we want to compare a set of items and look at rank or position, but they do not tell us anything about quantity. Ordinal numbers might, for example, be used to show us which speakers in a group spoke most often, or for the longest amount of time, and who came second, third, fourth etc., but they don't show us the differences in the *quantity* of speech produced by each speaker; in this sense ordinal scores carry less information than any counts on which they may be based. As such we need to be very careful when basing comparisons on ordinal numbers. They are only really useful when comparing members of the same group, and even then they aren't necessarily that informative in telling us about the differences between the members. Since they only give us the position they can be quite misleading. Take, for instance, the rank order of the number of utterances of eight speakers in a conversation. It might seem like a significant observation that a given speaker spoke fourth most often in a group of eight. But if the conversation was almost entirely dominated by speakers one, two and three, speaking fourth most often might not be very meaningful at all, and it would have been better to count the length of time for each speaker as a continuous variable. So, we need to be quite careful when dealing with ordinal numbers.

Examples of ordinal numbers include:

● Finishers in a race

● Positions in a league table

● Scaled responses to some questionnaires

When we use numbers in any kind of study it is vital that we are clear on which type of number we are using and what it is being used to achieve. Only once we are clear on this point can we progress to using numbers to describe our data.

> ## Q. Consider the examples below and identify the different uses of numbers based on the categories listed above.
>
> • There are four language classes named Class 1, Class 2, Class 3 and Class 4, each with 20 students. Classes 1 and 4 are for the under 18s, and Classes 2 and 3 are for adults.
>
> • There are three teachers: Classes 1 and 3 are taught by the same teacher using her own new method; Classes 2 and 4 are taught by two different teachers using the standard method.
>
> • Classes 1 and 2 have been studying for one year, and Classes 3 and 4 have been studying for two years.
>
> • On a standardised pronunciation test, classes scored the following average marks:
>
> Class 1 = 57%
>
> Class 2 = 44%
>
> Class 3 = 68%
>
> Class 4 = 75%

On this test, therefore, the 'league table' of the class performances is:

1   Class 4

2   Class 3

3   Class 1

4   Class 2

All students were set an essay question in which they were given a half hour to write. The number of words each student produced were:

Class 1 between 150 and 325 words

Class 2 between 175 and 310 words

Class 3 between 250 and 1000 words

Class 4 450 and 800 words

A. The types of number are indicated by their formatting.

italics = nominal

bold = continuous

<u>underlined = ordinal</u>

There are four language classes named Class *1*, Class *2*, Class *3* and Class *4*, each with **20** students. Classes *1* and *4* are for the under **18**s, and Classes *2* and *3* are for adults.

There are **three** teachers: Classes *1* and *3* are taught by the same teacher using her own new method; Classes *2* and *4* are taught by **two** different teachers using the standard method.

Classes *1* and *2* have been studying for **one** year, Classes *3* and *4* have been studying for **two** years.

On a standardised pronunciation test, classes scored the following average marks:

Class *1* = **57%**

Class *2* = **44%**

Class *3* = **68%**

Class *4* = **75%**

On this test, therefore, the 'league table' of the class performances is:

1   Class *4*

2   Class *3*

3   Class *1*

4   Class *2*

All students were set an essay question in which they were given a half hour to write. The number of words each student produced were:

Class *1* between **150** and **325** words

Class *2* between **175** and **310** words

Class *3* between **250** and **1000** words

Class *4* between **450** and **800** words

1.3.4 *Other ways of classifying numbers*

A *continuous* number – as defined above – may or may not include fractions. You may hear of types of numbers that do not include fractions: *natural* numbers, *whole* numbers and *integers*. The numbers 2, 3 and 4 are all integers, but 2.5, 3.23 and 4.999 are not. If you wish to learn more, these three types are defined in the glossary.

1.4 Converting nominal measures into continuous numbers

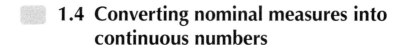

In some areas of life, measures are expressed as letters rather than numbers. This is particularly the case with methods of assessing student work. For example, assessment of student work is expressed at GCE A Level in the UK by letter, ranked from A (the best) through B, C, D, E, F and U, where U means unclassified and indicates a fail.

In the past, universities have also used letter grades to assess work, but now almost all assessment marks in UK universities are expressed as marks out of 100, for example:

Score/100	Grade
90–100	A – Outstanding
80–89	A – Excellent
70–79	A – Very good
60–69	B – Good
50–59	C – Sound
40–49	D – Pass
30–39	Fail
20–29	Fail
10–19	Fail
0–9	Fail

If you are faced with performance measures that are purely grades, and want to perform certain statistical tests on them (for example to work out the 'average' grade), then you may need to convert them to numbers.

Given the system in the table above, you might convert a grade D to 45%, a grade C to 55% and a grade B to 65% . . . but what would you do for the grade As and the fails? This is problematic, and you would be advised to work with the raw scores if they are available, rather than with the grades.

1.5 Fractions, decimals and percentages

Fractions, decimals and *percentages* represent the same thing: part of a whole.

It will be really useful for you to be familiar with switching between these three, specifically the following:

Fraction	Decimal	Percentage
1/2	0.5	50%
1/4	0.25	25%
1/10	0.1	10%
1/20	0.05	5%
1/100	0.01	1%
1/1000	0.001	0.1%
1	1.0	100%

Through this book you will see the following decimals quite often: 0.05 and 0.001.

Q: What is another way of saying 0.05?
A: 'One twentieth' or '1 in 20'.

Q: What is another way of saying $p < 0.05$? (Ignore for now what 'p' means.)
A: 'p is smaller than one in twenty'.

Q: What is another way of saying $p < 0.001$? (Ignore for now what 'p' means.)
A: 'p is less than one in a thousand'.

Why should you remember this? You will find out later.

 # 1.6 How you express probability with numbers

Another important concept for quantitative research is the notion of probability. *Probability* is the measure of the likelihood that an event will occur, that is, how likely it is that something *will* happen. Probability is quantified as a number between 0 and 1 (where 0 indicates impossibility and 1 indicates certainty). The higher the probability of an event, the more certain we are that the event will occur.

A useful definition of the idea of probability is that **the probability of event A is the number of ways event A can occur divided by the total number of possible outcomes**.

For example:

A spinner has four equal sectors coloured yellow, blue, green and red. When the spinner is spun, the probability of landing on any one of the four colours is one in four, so 1/4.

Another example is that of a six sided die. The probability of landing on any one of the numbers (1, 2, 3, 4, 5 or 6) is 1/6.

We can show probability on a **Probability Line**:

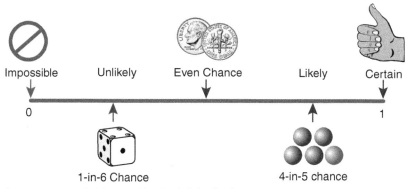

Source: www.mathsisfun.com/data/probability.html

Probability does not tell us exactly what will happen but is a guide as to what is likely to happen.

Q: If you toss a coin 100 times, how many times will heads come up?

A: Probability says that heads have a 1/2 chance, so we can **expect 50 heads**. But when we actually try it we might get 48 heads or 55 heads . . . or anything, really, but in most cases it will be a number near 50.

In the examples above, we have used fractions. In statistics, probability is usually expressed as a decimal rather than a fraction.

Q: In statistics, how would you write the probability of a die landing on a certain number?
A: 0.167.

Q: Is it exactly 0.167?
A: No – it is 0.1666666666666. . . (repeat the 6 as many times as you like). Here the figure is rounded to three decimal places.

Q: In statistics, how would you write the possibility that tomorrow's date will be the same as today's?
A: 0

Tossing a coin and throwing a die are examples of experiments. In linguistics research, experiments that are concerned with probability can be to do with the number of times certain words are likely to occur, the number of times different linguistic variables are used etc.

1.7 Summary

In this chapter, we have covered the basic concepts of **quantification** and **number**.

1. Numbers can be used as names or labels (like the number of a bus). These are *nominal* numbers. In statistical analyses they can be used to define categories, but they cannot be a feature that is statistically analysed.

2. *Continuous* numbers are numbers that can be analysed statistically (for example by being added together or averaged).

3. It is useful to know that 0.05 means 'one in twenty' and that 0.001 means 'one in a thousand'.

4. Probability is measured on a scale of 0 to 1 where 0 = impossible and 1 = certain.

1.8 References

Aliaga, M. and Gunderson, B. (2002). *Interactive statistics*. 2nd edition. Upper Saddle River, NJ: Prentice Hall.

Ernest, P. (2006). A semiotic perspective of mathematical activity: the case of number. *Educational Studies in Mathematics* 61 (1), 67–101.

2 Designing research projects which count things

2.1 Introduction: the dinner party experience

Research normally starts with an observation: something we might witness in our day-to-day lives or things we come across while reading that we find intriguing and want to find out more about. Let us say, for example, you are invited to a dinner party and have the impression during this particular evening that the female guests do almost all of the talking while the men keep comparatively quiet. You wonder whether this is how people communicate in general, or whether your dinner party experience is just a one-off. In other words, are we looking at a pattern? To establish a pattern in communicative practices would be an interesting research finding that might add to the growing body of knowledge that we have accumulated thus far on how people interact.

What do you do next as a student of linguistics? First, and most importantly, you look at research that has been done up to this point on the topic of gendered communicative practices in various contexts. You will find that there is a wealth of knowledge out there, and that you need to do a lot of reading first, because you do not want to reinvent the wheel with your own research project. While you are reading you notice that the researchers who wrote the books and articles on the subject of your interest went about their work in different ways: many base their findings on recordings of dinner table conversations which they then transcribe. Some look at only one transcription and analyse in meticulous detail how this particular piece of communication developed and how women and men interacted in it. This is qualitative research, focusing on one or a few representative examples of communication.

You as a student of linguistics might find all this fascinating, but you wonder whether such methods produce reliable results. Are they objective enough? Are they *scientific* enough? Do they generalise? To answer these questions you might think of turning to some more quantitative studies. But be careful. Before you look for a quantitative answer to your research question, some words of warning: numbers need not mean the research is any more objective or generalisable! Numbers can be used to lie and to manipulate audiences! In a famous scene in the film *Ghostbusters* (1984), Bill Murray's character, Pete Venkman, assures the mayor of New York that 'nearly 50% of us voted for you' in the last election. Given that there are four ghostbusters this of course means that only one of them voted for the mayor and three voted against! The humour in this case comes from our knowledge that the subversive Dr. Venkman is using statistics to spin what is actually a bad thing (that almost all of them voted against the mayor) so that it will be received in their favour. Not all misuses of statistics are funny or so harmless. In the case of Sally Clark, the mother wrongly convicted of killing her children, statistics were misapplied in court to give an overwhelming (and incorrect) impression of guilt. After her second son died of cot death, Mrs Clark was arrested – because of an assumption that having two children die of cot death in the same family was very unlikely. In the court case a paediatrician, Professor Roy Meadow, claimed that the chances of having two children die of cot death in the same (affluent) family was around 'one in 73 million'. This claim might have been true if there were no common causes between the two deaths, but it was later called into question. Two cot deaths in the same family home are probably not unrelated but may in fact have an underlying link that has not yet been established. Mrs Clark's conviction was eventually overturned by the court of appeal five years after her original arrest. In this case, the correct interpretation of statistics was absolutely crucial to the delivery of justice for Mrs Clark and her family.

But returning to our example of qualitative research: even in the qualitative analysis of only one transcribed dinner table conversation you might find some elements of quantitative analysis. While doing their qualitative analysis of male and female linguistic communicative practices at the dinner table, our qualitative researchers also tend to count: how often did men speak in this conversation, and how often did the women? Were there interruptions? How many? Who interrupted whom how often? Our qualitative analysis has clearly gone beyond the stage of observation and has raised our awareness of a number of linguistic and discursive features. Still, the question remains whether these features are common ones and could be part of a pattern. In order to answer this question we need to go beyond our first dinner table conversation and look at more similar ones.

Other researchers might then follow a different route of investigation and focus on questions such as turn taking and interruptions in conversations between men and women on a larger scale. They use larger data sets, for example by recording many instances of comparable communications so that their findings are not based on only one or two examples. The frequent recurrence of a phenomenon indicates that there might indeed be a pattern. The million-dollar question here is: how many occurrences of a specific phenomenon do we need to count before we can establish a pattern, and how large does our data set need to be?

Other researchers might have taken yet another route to find out about male and female communicative practices at the dinner table: they design questionnaires and ask people – men and women – about their experiences: is it true that women do more talking at the dinner table than men? Or is it the other way around? Depending on how many people respond to the questionnaire, these researchers get potentially large and interesting data sets. They can count the answers and present them in a quantitative way – for example in tables, graphs and diagrams – but it is important to keep in mind that what we got here is not necessarily the reality of communicative practices but people's perceptions of them.

Our little discussion of dinner table conversations has thrown up a number of issues to keep in mind before we design our research project:

- Quantitative and qualitative research are often interlinked.

- Quantitative research results are not necessarily more objective or more scientific than qualitative research. They focus on different aspects in the process of gaining knowledge.

- One of the major challenges of quantitative research is to establish how large a data set must be before it allows us to establish a linguistic pattern.

- When we base our quantitative research on questionnaires we get *perceptions* of linguistic realities, no more and no less.

Once you have decided that you want to include numerical data in your study you need to ensure that you design the project carefully so that the data you collect is useful. Before you start you need to think carefully about *what it is you want to count and why it is worth counting*. If you want to compare some numerical data you need to check that the comparison you are making is meaningful, and you need to consider whether any difference that you find is *significant*. At the most ambitious end of the scale you might be able to show a *statistically significant* difference between two sets of data, if you have designed your study in the right way to be able to use a *test of statistical significance* on your results. Design, then, is absolutely key. Above all else you must not rush into data collection without thinking through the *research design*. In this section we will discuss the key issues you need to be aware of when designing your project if you want to arrive at meaningful data, and perhaps even a statistically significant result.

2.2 Designing a quantitative research project

In the following sections we will introduce three examples of research projects that count things: a sociolinguistic survey, an attitudinal survey and a corpus linguistics project. We would like to begin with five steps for you to consider carefully before you start your data collection.

Step 1: Make sure that the data you need for your research isn't out there already.

In the age of the Internet we have access to an enormous wealth of data, so whatever it is that you are looking for might already be available.

But even if this is the case, your job as a researcher is not done: you still need to collect and analyse the data you find critically:

- On the basis of which underlying research design has the data been collected?
- Is it representative?
- Is the data set extensive enough?

A good data set should give answers to all the above questions.

Step 2: Formulate your research questions.

What exactly is it that you want to find out in your project?

Step 3: Decide what sort of data you need in order to answer your research questions.

Is it quantitative, qualitative or a mixture of both?

Step 4: Consider carefully which *method(s) of analysis* you will later apply to analyse your data.

It is important to think this through before starting to collect data, because different methods of analysis might need different forms of data.

Step 5: Decide which individuals or groups will make up your sample.

Who do you look for as potential informants?

How do you contact them?

Are there any ethical issues involved?

When tackling these steps, a crucial question to ask yourself is: what *type of study* am I doing? There are very distinct approaches that can be thought of as different types of research, and each comes with its own strengths and weaknesses – as well as a slightly different relationship with the use of numbers. Once you are aware which type of study it is that you want to do, you can also access the literature in a more focused way, developing a more in-depth understanding of the research method that you have chosen and the potential pitfalls that you need to look out for.

2.2.1 Do I need ethical approval?

Most universities will require students who collect data from specific individuals to get their informed consent, and most universities will require students to undergo a process of approval for projects that collect such data. Traditional ethical debates for linguistics researchers would focus on data collection by covert tape recording and whether, for example, this should be permitted if consent to use the recording in the research was obtained from the participants *after* the recording was made. More recent debates focus on what data can be legitimately scraped from the Internet and whether it makes a difference if one has to enter an area of the Internet using a login and password. For any research project you need to consider the ethics of the data collection and use, and this probably means discussing it with your tutor.

2.2.2 How much data do I need?

The question of sampling is discussed extensively in general research methods texts. In linguistics the issues will vary considerably between corpus linguists, who may wish to collect many millions of words of texts, and conversation analysts, who can content themselves with a hugely detailed analysis of relatively short stretches of tape. There is therefore no single answer to be given, but the questions you should consider include whether you want to generalise your results beyond the data collected, and if so in what way; and what kind of data you would need for it to be in some way representative of a wider population of texts. Is your main question descriptive – or do you want to make wider inferences from the language description which you produce? Depending on the answers to these kinds of questions, your sampling strategy may vary.

2.2.3 Do I need a hypothesis? Hypothesis testing and hypothesis generating

A typical worry that students often have is that they do not seem to have a hypothesis. Now, this might be a problem or it might not, and the key to figuring this out is working out which type of study you are doing. In hypothesis testing studies we are working in an area which is well established theoretically and empirically. This is because a field usually needs to be quite well developed before we can begin to formulate a hypothesis based on previous research and well-formed theories. Some of the questions to ask are: how well developed is the area I am working in? What is already known? What theories already exist? And – sometimes – what explicit hypotheses already exist in this area?

An example from linguistic research is the question of whether women use tag questions more often than men. Lakoff (1975) famously claimed that women do use tag questions more often than men in conversational situations. Notice that Lakoff has constrained the claim to a particular form of language (conversation). This is also a crucial aspect of working with hypothesis testing studies – the hypothesis needs to be carefully focused at the correct level of generalisation. Here we can express Lakoff's claim as a hypothesis: women use more tag questions in conversation than men. But a further problem here is that this is not just a famous claim but an old one – other studies have already tested and disputed this hypothesis in the past. Thus, Dubois and Crouch (1975) found that in 'at least one genuine social context, men did, and women did not, use tag questions' (p. 289). Later, Holmes (1984) claimed that the discourse function of the tag, and not merely the frequency of it, needed to be taken into account, claiming that the use of tag questions was associated with facilitators rather than non-facilitators. This rejection of the original hypothesis was later supported by Cameron, McAlinden and O'Leary (1989). In their study they provided evidence that the use of tag questions is a question of *power* rather than *gender*. In their data they showed that both powerless women and powerless men used tag questions more often than powerful women and powerful men. Over time, then, Lakoff's original hypothesis has thus been tested, refined and rejected. Now, when we are choosing a hypothesis it is clearly important to review the literature carefully to make sure that it hasn't already been refined, or even rejected repeatedly. When we start our research we need to try to be at or close to the 'cutting edge' of what is currently known; otherwise, we are in danger of doing pointless research, whilst simultaneously demonstrating our ignorance of what has already been done.

The other possibility, though, is that we might not want to do a hypothesis testing type of study at all. We might, for instance, be looking at a register or variety of language where little is known. In such a case we might not form a hypothesis at all. This might seem surprising, but in many areas of language studies, researchers start not with a hypothesis but with the attempt to *describe* and *explore* a set of data. In corpus linguistics, for example, a researcher would rarely if ever hypothesise as to what the most frequent words in a corpus might be, or what collocates a word might have; she would simply run the analysis and find out! This might lead to the generation of a hypothesis at a later stage, possibly as the conclusion of the project, based on patterns or regularities found in the data, but it wouldn't be the focus from the outset. Relatively new or emerging areas of language studies are often hypothesis generating rather than hypothesis testing, and it is always a good idea to think carefully about how established the field is that you are interested in when trying to decide whether your study should be hypothesis testing or hypothesis generating.

2.2.4 Do I need an experiment? Experimental versus non-experimental studies

Another key distinction in understanding what type of study you are doing is between experimental and non-experimental studies. There is sometimes a sense that a study is more 'scientific' if it is based on experimental data or if it can be 'proved' or replicated in experimental conditions. Linguistics, though, sits somewhat uncomfortably within scientific disciplines, since language use can be difficult to capture satisfactorily in controlled conditions without evoking the so-called observer's paradox that the linguistic practices of our informants will change the second we begin to observe them. Whilst there are ways around this through (carefully consented) covert or 'semi-covert' studies we need to think carefully about whether an experiment is appropriate at all when we are studying language. Perhaps the key factor is whether we are going to be able to get hold of the data that we want to study *without* using experimental methods. For many types of study it might be possible to collect authentic texts which will form data that allows us to investigate the feature we are interested in analysing. For example, this will often be the case for written data. There are fairly plentiful sources of data for newspaper articles, novels (especially those out of copyright and available in places like *Project Gutenberg*), websites, blogs, social media etc. When we want to carry out a study based on this kind of data we will rarely need to use experimental methods to collect them because so many authentic examples can be collected in a relatively efficient manner. For other types of study, though, such data may not be available. Indeed, this will often be the case for spoken data, where there is so much less available in the public domain than is the case for written language. If, for example, you wanted to study the way in which a certain word or words are pronounced in a region it would be incredibly time-consuming, and perhaps even impossible, to gather data just from existing data sets or random recordings. Instead, it would be necessary to 'trigger' the use of the target word(s) so that you can collect examples efficiently. This is the research aim behind Labov's famous 'fourth floor' study (1972), in which he asked shop assistants where he would find a certain item, chosen to elicit the response 'fourth floor' and thereby give him the phonological information he was seeking. This kind of targeted collection of elicited data can be useful in linguistics, enabling us to discover something that we can't easily access through the collection of texts or dialogues. However, when we are setting up our experimental conditions we will again have to be careful to ensure that the numbers we are eventually going to arrive at are going to be meaningful.

2.2.5 Case study or group study?

Finally, you need to think carefully about whether your overall research aims fit best with a *case study* or a *group study*. The key distinction here is very simple – are you going to be able to answer your research questions by looking in detail at one example (case study), or do you really need to compare a number of different sets of data to answer your question (group study)? If you are carrying out a case study you will need to think carefully about how you define the particular case that you want to analyse, so that the results that you arrive at are as useful and as generalisable as possible. The key questions to ask yourself are: is this example really worth looking at in great detail? Is it representative of the wider phenomenon that I want to examine, so that any findings I arrive at can be said to have a wider significance? Have the variables affecting my case study been taken into account so that my conclusions will be plausible? And, finally, does a close analysis of this case really meet the overall research aims of my study? For example, if you are interested in language and gender you might want to study the use of swear words by men and women, and perhaps you would investigate this by collecting tweets or recording spoken conversations. You might carry out a case study of a series of casual conversations involving a group of female participants in order to look for instances and frequencies of swearing. But you will need to carefully consider how representative your sample is in order to understand whether this is a good case study. Moreover, in order to answer your deeper research question, whether (and to what extent) swearing is a gender-related linguistic feature, you will of course need to carry out not just a case study but a comparative group study – since you won't be able to reach any conclusions unless you have a set of data from all-male participants with which to compare your findings from the all-female group.

For such a study you need to design your groups very carefully in order to make sure that the comparison that you want to make is valid. You will again need to consider any other variables besides gender that might be likely to affect the presence and frequency of swearing, and you will need to factor in these other variables when you attempt to make claims about the generalisability of your findings. The key thing to understand is that the similarities and differences between your two groups will need to be considered very carefully if your comparison is to be valid. In the case of your two gender groups, apart from the obvious difference of gender you would need the groups to be as similar as possible in terms of variables such as age and social class. You would also need to ensure that the contexts of the two sets of recordings are as similar as possible, for example in terms of the location of the conversations, the time of day they occurred, any prompts or structure you provided in order to set their interactions going and even (and perhaps especially) whether you allow the drinking of alcohol during these interactions. Some of these considerations might seem obvious, but it is surprisingly easy to overlook factors which might threaten the comparability of two groups, and this needs to be carefully avoided if any numbers that are produced from your study are really going to be comparable and thereby lead to a meaningful conclusion to your work.

In the following paragraphs we will look more closely at examples of linguistic research projects that include quantitative approaches, and we will talk you through the best ways to set them up. There are of course other ways to collect data for quantitative analysis, but we've tried to include some of those most used by students of linguistics.

2.3 Data collection example: working with questionnaires

It is obvious that not all people use language the same way, or that people don't use language in the same way all the time, depending on where they are and who they are communicating with. For an introduction to sociolinguistics see, for example, Coulmas (2013) or Holmes and Wilson (2017).

A typical sociolinguistic research question from the area of language variation and change, for example in relation to regional variation ('dialects'), could be whether people in a certain geographical area use the regional dialect. Let us assume that the data is not yet available (Steps 1 and 2). One way of answering this research question is to do a survey based on a questionnaire. Among our students we often observe an enthusiasm for this particular way of data collection, which is mostly based on the misconception that all you need to do is draft a number of questions and go out and find some people willing to answer them, in order to then present results in a pie chart. This approach, unfortunately, is a clear recipe for academic disaster: a sociolinguistic survey requires careful preparation and much thought in order to be a successful tool for data collection.

What are the gains of collecting data on the basis of a sociolinguistic survey? Conducting a survey by distributing a questionnaire will give you an overview of the sociolinguistic situation on the ground and would thus be a good way to approach the research question for our example (Step 3). However, you cannot simply distribute questionnaires at random. In our example – do people in a specific area use the local dialect? – you need to specify which part of the geographical area in question you are planning to survey, and you need to give the reasons for your decision. In an ideal world you would have a lot of money allocated to your project, which would allow you to employ researchers to cover the whole area where the dialect is supposed to be spoken. As a student you normally don't have these means, and you will need to find a representative geographical unit at a much smaller scale that would allow you to conduct your research and still come up with a meaningful result. You might want to look at a town or a village which, based on social statistics, allows you to claim that it is representative for the whole area. Importantly, you need to establish how many inhabitants this town or village has. If you are conducting a survey on linguistic practices in a geographical area your results are meaningful only if you cover a considerable percentage of its inhabitants, as a rule of thumb more than 20%. The question of sampling is comparatively easy in the case of our example: you would like to obtain filled-in questionnaires from as many inhabitants of the village as possible (Step 5).

There are various ways to approach your informants. You could, for example, consider publishing an article or an advert in the local newspaper, introducing yourself and the aims of your project and asking the villagers for their support. You need to be careful about the representativeness of your sample, however – for example, choosing to distribute a survey at a primary school in the village is likely to research younger adults (and miss older and retired residents), whereas distributing the same questionnaire at a day centre might have the opposite problem. It is important that you obtain your informants' written consent before they take part in your study. You need to assure your informants that you will safeguard their anonymity and will keep the data you collect safe at all times, for example by storing it on a password-encrypted computer.

A lot of thought and effort should go into the wording of your questionnaire. As Wray and Bloomer (2012: 166–167) put it:

> *The information you get will heavily depend on the way the questions are formulated and what choice, if any, you offer as possible responses. Thus, care must be taken not to unintentionally influence the findings by building assumptions into the formulation of the questions.*

We distinguish between open and closed questions: in the case of closed questions the answers are restricted by the questionnaire, for example by providing boxes to tick.

The following is an example of a closed question in the context of our example – the question whether people use the regional dialect:

Question: Do you understand the local dialect? YES / NO

This is an example of a simple YES/NO question. Another format would be *multiple choice questions* where your informants have more than two options to choose from:

Question: Which age group do you belong to? Please tick the box.
- ☐ 0–10
- ☐ 11–20
- ☐ 21–30 etc.

The results of closed questions are easy to count and to quantify.

Open questions can give your informants the opportunity to elaborate on a certain issue, as the example below shows:

> Question: Do you think the local dialect should be taught in schools? YES / NO
>
> Please explain your answer: _____
>
> _____
>
> _____

Open questions can give you interesting insights, but their results are difficult to count.

Your sociolinguistic survey of the village, if conducted carefully and based on a well-considered questionnaire, can provide you with interesting information, depending on the questions you ask in your questionnaire, such as the percentage of dialect speakers, their age, gender, educational background etc., which gives you a snapshot of the linguistic situation. In section 2.6 of this chapter we will explain in some detail how you can best describe your data.

But first we would like to draw your attention to a different questionnaire design that would allow you to find out more about the reasons behind the specific linguistic situation in the village. You can also ask questions about the informants' *attitudes*. When working with questionnaires we always need to keep in mind that the results we get are perceptions our informants have on certain issues. There are certain questions that do not allow too much scope for perception, for example questions about age or gender. However, even here there is room for ambiguity; for example, imagine surveying in a place of the world where no birth registers are kept and people simply don't know how old they are. If you would like to find out your informants' subjective reactions towards certain issues, you can, for example, use a *semantic differential scale*. It consists normally of a pair of adjectives with opposite meanings, at either end of a scale. Your informants can position themselves somewhere on the continuum between the two opposites:

> Stimulus: Knowledge of the local dialect is in your view. . .
>
> VITAL _ UNNECESSARY

Another scale that allows you to elicit your informants' subjective responses is the *Likert scale*. A statement expressing an attitude is given, and the informants indicate how strongly they agree or disagree with it:

Statement: Knowledge of the local dialect is vital.
very strongly agree – strongly agree – agree – neither agree nor disagree – disagree – strongly disagree – very strongly disagree

Both the semantic differential scale and the Likert scale are closed questions.

When using Likert scales it is important to design and use them correctly to ensure you are able to arrive at the best possible quantitative use of your results. One useful tip is to always use scales with 7 or more data points. If you set your scales up like this it then becomes possible to use what are known as *parametric statistics* on your results (more on these later). The crucial point to understand for now is that Likert scales with six or fewer points can *preclude the use of these statistics from the very start*. There will be no way for you to go back and 'fix' the data at a later stage – if you decided you wanted to use parametric statistics you would need to start the entire study again. This is a crucial point about the move from numbers to statistics. If it is our ambition to arrive at statistically significant results we need to plan for them from the very start.

A second crucial issue with use of the Likert scale is how you use the scales once you have collected your results. Newcomers to the field of quantitative analysis sometimes assume that it is possible to 'add up' the results of a Likert scale study to arrive at an overall score. This is problematic because it treats each of the answers on the scale as though it is somehow equal to the others and that the numbers arrived at are equivalent and can be added or subtracted in the way that we would usually manipulate continuous numbers – but this is quite wrong. If we think back to what we said earlier when we discussed what a number is, the problem here is that *ordinal* numbers are being treated as if they were *continuous* numbers.

Finally, it is often (though not always) considered to be good practice to have an even number of positions in your Likert scale. This removes the possibility of a respondent unthinkingly picking the middle answer! If there is an even number of points on the scale there is no middle option and the respondent is forced to make a choice; this can mean they think a little more carefully about where to place their response. On the other hand, this also rules out a neutral answer to a question on which the respondent may truly be indifferent! So, if you ask a question on which your subject has absolutely no feeling one way or another, the most accurate position for their answer would arguably be the middle point – but if you have removed this middle point by having an even number of places you have forced them to choose one way or the other. This perhaps shows us some of the limitations of the Likert scale system. Whilst it can be very useful it is always a somewhat artificial exercise to turn opinions and feelings into numbers.

You can also apply the Likert scales for a more experimental research design in order to find out more about your informants' attitudes, for example towards the local dialect. If you conduct an experiment you could, for example, play a number of recordings of the local dialect in use – read aloud, spontaneous, in different genres etc. – to your informants and ask them to note down their reaction to the recording on a Likert scale:

Stimulus: Recording of a poetry reading in the local dialect
Statement: I enjoy listening to the poem in the local dialect.
very strongly agree – strongly agree – agree – neither agree nor disagree – disagree – strongly disagree – very strongly disagree

2.4 Data collection example: the experimental approach

The experimental approach tends to be used when it would otherwise be very difficult to gather relevant data. In linguistics this usually means some form of 'elicitation' – the use of a technique to trigger a respondent to produce the target language that you want to study. Studies in linguistics have tended to fall into two main categories – the discourse completion test (DCT) and the role-play (Jucker 2009). In the former type the researcher creates a stretch of speech or writing (the *discourse*) with a gap in it. The elicitation technique then works by presenting the respondent with the discourse, which acts as a cue, and noting down or recording the response. Whilst such tasks can often be very artificial and perhaps encourage participants to produce language of a type that they might not naturally engage in, they do allow us to access data that might otherwise be impossible to collect. Jucker (2009) provides an interesting discussion of the role of experimental data in the body of research related to the paying of compliments. Whilst compliments are a familiar feature of discourse, it can be difficult to capture them, and they will not necessarily occur as a matter of course when a researcher begins to record. Indeed, Jucker et al. (2008) report that there are just 343 compliments in the entire 110 million word British National Corpus. This kind of scarcity of a linguistic feature in naturally occurring data is often used as a justification for the experimental approach, but there are again a number of factors that need to be carefully considered. First, the elicitation technique should be as natural as possible. Ideally, it should put the respondent into a situation with which they are familiar and lead to them producing discourse of a kind that they might normally produce. If a DCT is to be used, the trigger language needs to be as neutral as possible so that a range of possibilities are open to the respondent, rather than leading them to a particular type of answer. To return to our example of compliments, a DCT to collect compliments might look like this:

> You meet an acquaintance you haven't seen for some time. After an exchange of greetings, s/he says: 'You look so nice! Even nicer than when I saw you last'. To this, you reply: . . .
>
> (Chen 1993, reproduced in Jucker 2009)

The format of the DCT is instructive. The respondent is given a context and some relevant text that acts as a cue. Even the form of words, though, creates difficulties – what if your respondent doesn't have an acquaintance whom they think might talk like this? But the idea is that the experience will be familiar enough to provoke a response, which can then be measured. How, though, can this lead to quantifiable data? In other words, what is there here that we can count?

An example of an experimental role-play is given by Grant and Macleod (2016), whose broader study is into the language used between paedophiles and their child victims in online chat rooms. The real world data in this language context is very difficult to work with so they created a proxy data set from role-plays through which they could study identity formation in online chat. Their role-plays had different degrees of closeness to their naturally occurring data set. The role-plays thus varied from students chatting through Yahoo Messenger about a series of everyday topics to simulated sexualised chat performed by real online police officers as part of their training. In this way the researchers were able to elicit the data they needed to analyse for their study.

The results of experimental studies like this might well give us data in the form of numbers but not until the responses have been recorded and categorised. If there is a very narrow range of possible responses (for example if there are yes/no type questions or if the discourse task elicits a binary response where respondents can say one of two types of things) it is relatively simple to turn our results into numbers. We can simply count the number of responses that fell into either of the two possibilities and then compare the numbers. However, if there is a wide range of possible responses, such as in a role-play scenario, it will be a much more complex process to categorise the results in a way that translates into numbers. We will need to design a framework for analysis to cluster different catego-ries of responses carefully, making sure that our choices are well justified and our overall categories are well defined. If they are, and if we can demonstrate that we are being consistent, we can count and compare the different types of responses given, providing quantitative data that provides evidence about a particular linguistic practice. There are dangers, though, and a good rule of thumb is that we should always compare the results of experimental studies to those generated through more natural methods (such as through corpus work) in order to see whether the elicited data is sufficiently similar to that found in 'real' encounters.

2.5 Data collection example: working with corpus data

Collecting relatively large amounts of naturally occurring language data in a corpus has become a popular research method in applied linguistics. Through the use of corpus analysis software such as AntConc, Wordsmith Tools and Sketch Engine it is possible to search for items and patterns in large bodies of text quickly in order to make observations about language which might otherwise be difficult or impossible. It might not surprise you that *the* is the most frequent word form in the English language, but how many times do you think it typically occurs in every 1000 words? What are the 20 most frequent words in the English language? What are the most fre-quent lexical words? Whether at a general level (when trying to talk about a language as a whole) or a specific level (when speculating about a particular register or variety) it is incredibly difficult to answer such questions intuitively. This is where corpus linguistics becomes a useful approach. A corpus is defined as 'a collection of naturally-occurring language text, chosen to characterise a state or variety of language' (Sinclair 1991: 171). As Sinclair states, it involves not experimental data but naturally occurring language – examples of authentic language use such as newspaper articles, novels, political manifestos or spoken conversations. From a research design point of view the crucial aspect of this definition is the word *characterise* in the quote from Sinclair: how will you collect a set of authentic texts that are representative of the state or variety that you want to study? This is a much trickier question than it might seem at first because there are so many variables that affect the linguistic features found in examples of actual language use. Let's say that you want to compare the language of men to the language of women – which is a very general starting point. Which texts can you collect to represent women and men? Are these texts solely by women or men, or might they involve some collaboration? What type of texts will you choose, and can you get the same type of text for both men and women? How many different men and women will you need to sample so that you can try to *generalise* about each gender from the data, rather than just describing the possibly idiosyncratic features of a small group of each that might not be typical of the gender as a whole? Is it even possible to represent a whole gender? Or do we need to take into account different ages, social classes and geographical locations? What about if we are collecting data from writers (or speakers) whose first language is not English? Should we exclude them or include them? If we're going to arrive at meaningful numbers when we analyse a corpus we will need to have planned carefully, taking these kinds of factors into consideration.

Above all else, we will need to look carefully at the literature, assessing how similar studies have been done. What corpora have been used by professional academics to represent our variety? How many texts and how many types of text did they include? How did they try to account for the many variables that can affect language in order to isolate the particular state or variety that they wanted to study? This might be very difficult, or it might be quite easy. In Mahlberg's (2015) study of stylistics in the work of Charles Dickens her corpus is simply everything written by Dickens. This can be seen as being *maximally representative* in the sense that she has collected everything that exists (as far as we know). It is a fairly small corpus, but it is everything that Dickens wrote and so it represents Dickens fully. It is quite possible to create such corpora even in the limited time available for an undergraduate project or dissertation, and it is quite an exciting thought to realise that you are working with the same exact data set that a professional academic attempting your study would use.

There is further good news in that once we have carefully collected a corpus that is representative of the state or variety that we want to study, arriving at some accurate numbers is very straightforward. Most suites of corpus linguistics software have a wordlist function in which a *tokenizer* identifies all of the different word forms (or *types*) in a corpus and gives their frequencies at the touch of a button. No counting of items by the researcher is necessary for this, removing the possibility of human error from the process. This process is also incredibly quick (indeed, it is almost instantaneous), meaning that we can arrive at a great deal of highly reliable quantitative data from a large data set in seconds. Once we begin to reach this point, when we have moved from words to numbers, we need to think about how we will describe our data.

2.6 Describing your data

Once we are clear on what nominal, continuous and ordinal numbers are used for we can think about how we can use numbers to *describe* data. Here we are thinking about how we can describe, show or summarise our data in order to make our findings clearer or more meaningful, and ultimately see any patterns more clearly. Two descriptive tools that are key to making sense of quantitative data are the ability to calculate the *average* and the *measure of spread* of a set of results.

2.6.1 Calculating the average – but which average?

There are three ways of calculating an average: *mean*, *median* and *mode*. Each of these can give different results, and they represent three different ways of conceptualising what counts as the average in a set of numbers. Consider the following example, a set of nine marks from a final-year university student.

58   58   58   67   68   72   80   85   85

One way that we can calculate the average is to calculate the *mean* value. To do this we add up all of the values and then divide them by the total number of instances. So we calculate the total number by adding up all of the results:

$$58 + 58 + 58 + 67 + 68 + 72 + 80 + 85 + 85 = 631$$

And then we divide this by the number of instances (9) to give us our mean:

$$631 \div 9 = 70.11$$

So the average mark of this student when using the mean is 70.11.

Second, instead of the mean we can find the *mode*. This is the most commonly found result and can be understood as the average in the sense that it is the result that the student gets most often. So, to find this, we identify the most common value present. If we look back through the nine marks we can see that 58 is the most common (occurring three times), whilst 85 occurs only twice and each of the other results occurs only once. The mode, then, is 58: quite a big drop from 70.11!

Finally, we can look at the *median*. The median conceptualises the averages as the middle value of a set. In order to find the median we need to order the results from lowest to highest (as they appear above) and then identify the middle value. The middle of nine values is the fifth, meaning that the median for this student is 68. So, depending on whether we take the mean, the median or the mode, the average for this student can be seen as being 58, 68 or 70.11 – quite an important range of differences when it comes to deciding on a final degree classification! What this shows is that we need to think carefully about how we want to conceptualise the average and we need to be aware that the three ways of calculating this can result in quite different outcomes.

The technical term for the type of average chosen is the **measure of central tendency**. When we decide to answer any question involving an average we need to consider which measure of central tendency we want to use, and this simply means deciding whether we want to use the *mean*, the *median* or the *mode*. We might even look at two or even all three of these and compare them, as we did above, in order to check how representative each of them appears to be.

2.6.2 Measures of spread

A useful concept when considering averages is the *measure of spread.* This is because, as the example of the student marks in the previous section showed, the average only tells us part of the story and can even be misleading depending upon which type of average, or measure of central tendency, is chosen and how consistently the values (marks, in this case) are spread out around that average. When we come to compare the average of one group of values to another this problem becomes even more crucial. Knowing that the *mean* of one group is higher than that of another does not tell you enough to work out whether there is a difference between the two groups.

Take a look at these averages.

	Student 1	Student 2
Mean	70.11	70.11

On the face of it, it looks as though these students have performed very similarly. The average figures tell us part of the story but not all of it. We need to know: 'Were most of the scores clustered quite close to the average figure, or were they spread out more widely?' In the case of Student 1 we know that they are spread out quite widely – but what about the scores for Student 2? These are as follows:

$$62 \quad 68 \quad 68 \quad 70 \quad 70 \quad 70 \quad 71 \quad 72 \quad 83$$

Straightaway we can see that the spread of marks for Student 2 is much smaller than for Student 1. All but two of the marks gained by Student 2 is within four marks of the mean. Student 2 has therefore been more consistent than Student 1. But how can we calculate a value for the amount of spread that allows us to make a more exact comparison between the two? The figures that tell us this are called **measures of spread.** The simplest measure of spread is just **the range**. The range is the difference between the highest number and the lowest number for each student. The range for Student 1 is 27 (85 minus 58) and for Student 2 is 21 (83 minus 62). The range can be a useful measure, particularly if the mean and the median scores are very different from each other; if the mean and median scores are close to each other, there are better measures of spread to use called the **variance** and the **standard deviation**. In our case the median scores are 68 for Student 1 and 70 for Student 2, and these are both close to the means of 70.11, so it makes sense to calculate variances and standard deviations. You should use these if you can because they give you more information than a simple range, as we shall see in later chapters.

You can calculate both variance and standard deviation using spreadsheets or a statistical software package such as SPSS. To really understand what these measures are, however, it is useful to see how easily they can be calculated. The calculation for the standard deviation takes in the calculation of variance along the way.

Here are the steps:

1. Work out the mean of the numbers.

   For Student 1 the mean is 70.11.

2. Then for each number subtract the mean from each score.

   For Student 1

   $$58 - 70.11 = -\textbf{12.11}$$

   $$58 - 70.11 = -\textbf{12.11}$$

   $$58 - 70.11 = -\textbf{12.11}$$

   $$67 - 70.11 = -\textbf{3.11}$$

   $$68 - 70.11 = -\textbf{2.11}$$

   $$72 - 70.11 = \textbf{1.89}$$

   $$80 - 70.11 = \textbf{9.89}$$

   $$85 - 70.11 = \textbf{14.89}$$

   $$85 - 70.11 = \textbf{14.89}$$

3. For each of these numbers you need to calculate the square by multiplying it by itself. You'll notice that by doing this we turn a mixture of positive and negative numbers into a list of positive numbers.

   For Student 1

   $$-12.11^2 = -12.11 \times -12.11 = \textbf{146.65}$$

   $$-12.11^2 = \textbf{146.65}$$

$-12.11^2 = \mathbf{146.65}$

$-3.11^2 = \mathbf{9.67}$

$-2.11^2 = \mathbf{4.45}$

$1.89^2 = \mathbf{3.57}$

$9.89^2 = \mathbf{97.81}$

$14.89^2 = \mathbf{221.71}$

$14.89^2 = \mathbf{221.71}$

4. The next step is to calculate the mean of all of these answers. The single number that results is sometimes referred to as 'the mean of the sum of squares', but the common name for it is **variance**, and it can be used as a useful measure of spread in some circumstances.

   For Student 1 the sum of squares, or variance, of her scores is 998.87.

   $146.65 + 146.65 + 146.65 + 9.67 + 4.45 + 3.57 + 97.81 + 221.71$
   $+ 221.71 = 998.87$

   $998.87 \div 9 = 110.99$

5. Finally, the **standard deviation** is calculated by taking the square root of the variance. This returns the number to a similar scale as for the original scores.

   For Student 1

   $\sqrt{110.99} = 10.54$

If we then calculate the standard deviation for Student 2 we find that the variance is 29.65 and the standard deviation is 5.54. In both cases this represents that the spread of Student 2's scores is less than the spread of Student 1's scores.

2.7 Designing a study so that a statistical test is possible

Finally, it is important to understand the relationship between the careful design of your data collection and the possibility of using statistics. In common parlance we talk of statistics as almost any numerical data, particularly when talking about claims in the news media, such as the one reported here:

> A *British Journal of Cancer* study showed that people who eat an extra 50 grams of processed meat (the equivalent of a sausage) a day can raise the risk of the condition by 19 percent, and people who ate an extra 100 grams of processed meat a day can raise their risk by 38 percent.
>
> (*Huffington Post*, July 3, 2013)

In this example percentage figures are being given for the increased risk of pancreatic cancer among people who engage in two activities (eating an extra 50 grams of processed meat per day and eating an extra 100 grams of processed meat per day). The figures seem quite large (19% and 38%), but what we are not told (here at least) is what the risk is in the first place. So, if the risk is vanishingly small, increasing it by 19% or even 38% may not concern people too much. On the other hand, if the risk is quite large, this finding might lead people to think again about their relationship with bacon and salami. What this shows, then, is the care that we need to take when collecting and illustrating quantitative data if our statistics are going to be meaningful. In order to see how we can plan for this successfully it is useful to be aware of the distinction between *descriptive* and *inferential* statistics.

2.7.1 *What is meant by* descriptive *and* inferential *statistics?*

When we use the term *descriptive statistics* we refer to, as the name suggests, the different ways in which we can *describe* our data, which that were outlined in section 2.6.

2.7.2 *Moving on: from descriptive statistics to inferential statistics*

One of the biggest misconceptions about statistical testing is that it can be added on at the end of a study, almost as an afterthought, in order to see how useful the findings are. This kind of thinking is very common, but unfortunately it is wrongheaded. Most frustratingly, it often leads to studies that contain very interesting insights and promising quantitative material but to which no statistical test can be applied. The reason for this is quite simple – **in order for statistical tests to be useful in a study, the data collection needs to be designed in the right way from the very start**. You can think of this as a set of rules for each statistical test; rules which need to be obeyed if you are going to be able to use a test at all.

Further to this, statistical tests can vary in their **power** to find a result. For example, a more powerful statistical test for comparing two groups of numbers will be able to detect a smaller difference between those groups than a less powerful test. If you collect data so that it falls into **normal distributions** this usually allows you to conduct more powerful tests. A test called a *t*-test is more powerful in detecting differences between data sets than an alternative called the Mann-Whitney U test. But a *t*-test is ideally used on normally distributed data, so a Mann-Whitney U test will be useful where this is not the case. An associated idea around this idea of the power of a test is that of different sorts of error. A Mann-Whitney U test might miss a difference that a *t*-test could detect. Missing a possible difference through a lack of power is called a Type 2 statistical error. The opposite, a Type 1 statistical error, would be an assertion that there was a difference between two groups of numbers when in fact this was not the case.

When you are thinking of using a statistical test it is important to understand that they are not used to prove an assertion but rather to reject what is called **the null hypothesis**. The assertion or hypothesis being tested might be that there is a difference between two groups. For example, an assertion or hypothesis may state that men and women differ in their judgements of the sexiness of Klingon as a language. A statistical test cannot demonstrate (from your data) that this is true. You can, however, use a statistical test to demonstrate that the null hypothesis, that there is no difference between the judgements of the two groups, is very unlikely to be true. If the statistical test allows you to make that assertion then you are allowed to say that because you are happy to reject the null hypothesis – that there is no difference – you are happy to accept the experimental or alternative hypothesis – that there is a difference between the two groups.

2.8 What do we mean by data?

It is helpful at this point to clarify how we are using the word *data* as this can sometimes be ambiguous. Drawing on arguments from Coombs (1964), some researchers will refer to both their recorded observations or collected samples and their later analysis, too, as data. This can cause confusion, so here, in terms of undertaking quantitative analysis, we will use the term *data* when the sample of written or spoken language has actually been classified in some way, into categories from which inferences might be made. So, rather than referring to a recording or a transcript alone as a form of data, we can think of these collected samples of language as a basis for extracting data, which you, as an analyst, will then describe quantitatively (Macaulay 2009: 19).

It is helpful to think in this way because, if we consider what a transcript of a recording may contain, an analyst may not necessarily include all elements. They may be selective within their wider methodological framework and in relation to literature they have reviewed. In some forms of linguistic analysis, perhaps where people are studying conversation, much more of the transcript may be closely examined than in other scenarios, where pauses and laughter, for example, may not be of much interest. Whatever your chosen area of focus, in order to describe your words with numbers you will need to order them in some way.

 ## 2.9 Summary

Quantitative and qualitative research are often interlinked.

1. **Before** collecting data (a) check whether data exists already and, if it does, use that instead of collecting more; (b) define exactly how you will analyse it, so you collect the right amount in the right way; and (c) define how you will sample.

2. A study in a well-defined area of research may seek to test a hypothesis. A study in a less well-explored area may not have a hypothesis to test but will instead aim to describe data in order to generate hypotheses that can be tested in the future.

3. Data may be gathered in an experimental way or may be openly available. Openly available spoken data is harder to find than written data.

4. Experimental data collection methods include DCTs and role-plays.

5. The issue of representativeness and validity is important when considering both case studies and group studies.

6. Questionnaires can only elicit *perceptions* of linguistic realities.

7. When asking questions using a Likert (or other) scale, you must use a scale with at least 7 points if you plan to apply parametric statistical tests.

8. Corpus analysis tools afford relatively simple and powerful ways to analyse large collections of language data.

9. For a description of data sets to be meaningful, you need to give a *measure of spread* as well as an *average*.

2.10 References

Cameron, D., McAlinden, F. and O'Leary, K. (1989). Lakoff in context: the social and linguistic functions of tag questions. In J. Coates and D. Cameron (eds.), *Women in their speech communities*. Longman: London, 74–93.

Chen, R. (1993). Responding to compliments: a contrastive study of politeness strategies between American English and Chinese speakers. *Journal of Pragmatics* 20, 49–75.

Coombs, C.H. (1964). *A theory of data*. New York: Wiley.

Coulmas, F. (2013). *Sociolinguistics: the study of speakers' choices*. Cambridge: Cambridge University Press.

Dubois, B.L. and Crouch, I. (1975). The question of tag questions in women's speech: they don't really use them, do they? *Language in Society* 4, 289–294.

Grant, T. and MacLeod, N. (2016). Assuming identities online: experimental linguistics applied to the policing of online paedophile activity. *Applied Linguistics* 2, 50–70.

Holmes, J. (1984). Hedging your bets and sitting on the fence: some evidence for hedges as support structures. *Te Reo* 27, 47–62.

Holmes, J. and Wilson, N. (2017). *An introduction to sociolinguistics*. 5th edition. New York: Routledge.

Jucker, A.H. (2009). Speech act research between armchair, field and laboratory: the case of compliments. *Journal of Pragmatics* 41, 1611–1635.

Jucker, A.H., Schneider, G., Taavitsainen, I. and Breustedt, B. (2008). Fishing for compliments: precision and recall in corpus-linguistic compliment research. In A.H. Jucker and I. Taavitsainen (eds.), *Speech acts in the history of English* (Pragmatics & Beyond New Series 176). Amsterdam: Benjamins, 273–294.

Labov, W. (1972). *Sociolinguistic patterns*. Philadelphia: University of Philadelphia Press.

Lakoff, R. (1975). *Language and woman's place*. New York: Harper & Row.

Mahlberg, M. (2015). *Corpus stylistics and Dickens's fiction*. London: Routledge.

Macaulay, R. (2009). *Quantitative methods in sociolinguistics*. New York: Palgrave Macmillan.

Sinclair, J.M. (1991). *Corpus, concordance, collocation*. Oxford: Oxford University Press.

Wray, A. and Bloomer, A. (2012). *Projects in linguistics and language studies: a practical guide to researching language*. 3rd edition. London: Hodder.

Asking and answering quantitative questions

In the first part of this book we considered the notion of numbers, systems of counting, and different categories and ways of classifying numbers. In Chapter 2 you learned about methods of designing a quantitative research project and understanding the kind of study you are doing. If you were undertaking a *qualitative* analysis of words, then you might be describing certain features of your language sample, with examples and an analysis of meaning, but in *quantitative* research, such linguistic features are classified and counted, so you literally describe the words in your sample with numbers!

In this part we provide an overview of the process of carrying out quantitative research, that is, how you should go about asking, and answering, research questions that involve numbers. As an example, we will review this process first by looking at a project examining participants' attitudes to the sound of the artificial Klingon language and how erotic they find the language. The idea is to demonstrate the analysis process that you will go through in doing quantitative research. The following questions and answers follow a similar structure or consider just one part of the process. The overall research process can be broken down into a number of discrete stages.

1. **Read the literature to develop a research story.** Sometimes there will be a lot of literature and your study will essentially be a repetition

(or replication) of previous work. Sometimes your own study will be a response to the literature – taking previous work and tweaking it slightly or pointing out there is a gap in the previous literature. The purpose of this stage is to arrive at an interesting research question.

2. **Design your study to collect the numerical data.** Deciding that your question will best be answered through a quantitative design or at least a research design that involves using some quantitative methods should be a very conscious process. You need to be able to explain the advantages of taking a quantitative approach. Having made this decision, you need to deal with all the considerations discussed in Chapter 2.

3. **Collect the data.** This can be very time-consuming and involve all sorts of smaller design decisions which need to be recorded. It should not be confused with 'doing the research', as doing the research involves all of the stages.

Up until this point you've not done any quantitative analysis – the quantitative analysis comprises three main stages: describing the data with numbers and pictures and then drawing statistical conclusions.

4. **Describe and explore your quantitative data with numbers.** This means calculating appropriate measures of central tendency (averages) and measures of spread. The idea in doing this is to explore and understand your data better.

5. **Describe and explore your quantitative data with pictures.** This introduces the world of visualisation, graphs and charts. Visual representations of data are so much easier to read than tables of numbers. They are useful not only for summarising a data set but also for exploring that set for patterns. By using visualisations you can sometimes see things in the data that were not apparent before. One important pattern to look for is whether the data falls into a **normal distribution**. This is described in more detail in the examples.

It may be that you are carrying out a purely descriptive project; if so, you may not reach the next stage of analysis. That is okay. Not every quantification requires inferential statistical tests to be applied.

6. **Draw statistical conclusions from the data using inferential tests.** The purpose of most inferential tests is to ask a question of the data so

that you can draw some kind of generalisation with some degree of certainty. This might be a generalisation about an association between two data sets or a difference between two data sets, or you might be interested in some other kind of question.

7. **Relate these statistical conclusions back to the research story you have developed from the literature.** This is a final crucial stage of your investigation – the statistical conclusions have a wide meaning only as part of the more general research story you are developing, and they can be understood and interpreted properly only in the context of that story.

Survey of the sexiness of Klingon

Is your data *normal*?

3.1 The research story

There are a number of linguistic studies which examine regional responses to accents or other linguistic features (see Garrett 2010 for a broad discussion), and some of these look at gendered responses. Coupland and Bishop (2007), for example, show that women tend to have a more positive attitude to accents which are different from their own than do men, but their data also seems to imply an 'anchor' effect. This means that accents that are close to your own attract different positive or negative evaluations than accents that are more different. In this study we wanted to look at how sexy or erotic language sounds where there could be no anchor effect. Instead of picking a variety of English – or a foreign language which some participants might have some knowledge of – we chose to examine responses to the fictional language of Klingon.

3.2 Designing the study to collect numerical data

We decided to use a single 10-point scale to measure how erotic participants found Klingon where a score of 1 meant 'not at all erotic' and a score of 10 meant 'extremely erotic'.

We decided on a 10-point scale rather than a 3-, 5-, 7- or 9-point scale for two reasons. First, this bigger number makes the data drawn from the scale closer to a continuous scale. In contrast, 3-point scales and 5-point scales might be considered ordinal data at best. Some researchers argue that scales with 7 or more points can be treated as continuous, and we wanted to be on the safe side of that line.

Second, we wanted to force participants into a choice. We didn't want them to be able to choose a midpoint on the scale, and with an even-numbered scale there is of course no midpoint.

 ## 3.3 Data collection

We recruited 79 people (35 male, 44 female) who listened to an alien conversation between a male and female Klingon and then rated how erotic they found the language on the 1 to 10 scale.

These are the raw data:

male	5	male	4	female	6
male	6	male	5	female	6
male	7	male	4	female	1
male	9	male	7	female	4
male	7	male	8	female	7
male	3	male	6	female	4
male	3	male	6	female	8
male	10	male	4	female	5
male	9	female	1	female	5
male	9	female	4	female	6
male	7	female	9	female	5
male	8	female	6	female	3
male	6	female	8	female	1
male	5	female	5	female	7
male	8	female	1	female	9
male	7	female	5	female	7
male	8	female	4	female	6
male	7	female	5	female	5
male	6	female	3	female	7
male	4	female	6	female	4
male	8	female	0	female	6
male	3	female	2	female	3
male	7	female	2	female	2
male	9	female	5	female	8
male	7	female	5	female	6
male	5	female	4		
male	6	female	2		

One of the first things you notice is that it is very hard to see any useful patterns in data presented in this way. This is why we need to first describe the data with numbers and then with pictures.

 # 3.4 Describing the data with numbers

In describing the data with numbers we will first look at the measures of central tendency (or averages), then the measures of spread; finally, we will look at whether the data falls into a regular pattern called a normal distribution.

3.4.1 Averages

Averages are useful measures that can help us build a story about the frequency counts. Chapter 2 has already explained the concept of averages, but a recap with a view to this Klingon data is useful. Whilst most people have an idea of what the term *average* means, for example to summarise a large amount of data, or to indicate where there is variability within this data, in mathematics there are three different definitions of average.

Let's look at the mean, mode and median by examining the Klingon ratings more closely.

The averages are:

	Female	Male
Mean	4.70	6.37
Median	5	7
Mode	5	7

Just to recap, the mean is the average you get by adding all the scores and dividing by the number of scores, the median is the score that is in the middle once you have rank ordered them all, and the mode is the most frequently occurring score.

If you don't know which type of average to quote with your data, here's what to think through:

When should I use this average?	Measure of central tendency
When the numbers in the responses are continuous and evenly spaced out – that is, there are no great outliers.	Mean

When should I use this average?	Measure of central tendency
When the numbers in the responses have great outliers – for example if you have a list of salaries in a company, the salaries of the highest executives may be outliers.	Median
When you want to know the most common or most popular category. More rarely useful than the other two measures.	Mode

An outlier is a score that is a kind of statistical one-off. In our Klingon data no man scored the language as less erotic than a 3, so a man who scored the sample as a 1 might be considered an outlier, but this is probably not extreme enough. A rough and ready way to see from the numbers (rather than from a graph) whether your data has outliers is to check whether the mean is close to the median. If this is the case there are probably no outliers. In our case, for both groups the means and the medians are close. This is gives us confidence to quote the mean as the best measure of central tendency.

Q: Looking at the Klingon data, what do these averages tell you?
A: Klingon was liked more by males than by females.

Q: Great! So that's a result, then?
A: Not really. Read on . . .

3.4.2 Measures of spread: variance and standard deviation

Knowing that the mean of one group is higher than that of another does not tell you enough to work out whether there is a difference between the two groups. Take a look at these averages again:

	Female	Male
Mean	4.70	6.37

The average figures tell us part of the story but not all of it. We need to know: 'were most of the scores clustered quite close to the average figure, or were they spread out more widely?'

As described in Chapter 2 a figure that is useful to tell us this is the **standard deviation**. You can calculate it using software such as Excel or SPSS. These are the figures for our Klingon data:

	Female	Male
Mean	4.70	6.37
Standard deviation	2.32	1.90

The standard deviation is there to tell us how spread out the scores are. In this case, we can see that the scores are spread out rather more for the women than for the men. It is worth thinking about the relationships between the means and standard deviations, so one thing to notice is that the distance between the two means is about one standard deviation. This suggests that there is some separation between the two groups but also some overlap.

This will become more apparent when we start to graph the data.

3.5 Describing the data with pictures

It is important to carry out a variety of visualisations on your data to explore it to the fullest. In the Klingon study we have a comparison between two groups. This means we might want to look at some visualisations which compare the two groups and others which take each group on its own. This book deliberately does not recommend any particular piece of software for carrying out analyses or producing graphs, but in this section we've used SPSS, a piece of statistical software that is available in many universities.

3.5.1 Boxplots

One of the most useful starting places for a comparison between two groups is a boxplot.

By default, SPSS creates boxplot graphs that are based on the median score rather than a mean and draws the boxes to include 25% of the scores above and below the median. SPSS uses this as a default because it is probably the most useful boxplot to draw.

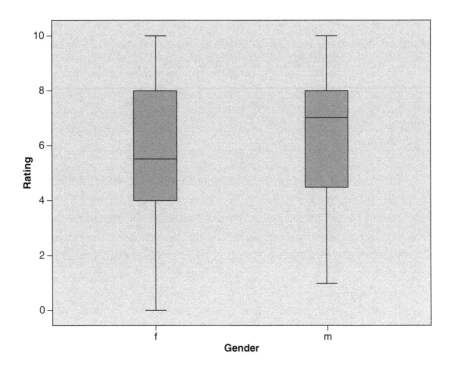

Here, the thick line in the middle of each box represents the median, and the box for each gender represents 50% of the responses (a quarter in the area above the median line and a quarter in the area below it). The lines from the end of each box represent the range of scores.

Q: What does this boxplot tell you about the difference between the males and females?
A: There doesn't seem to be much difference between the males and females. The difference in the medians looks less important now that it has been put in the context of the spread.

Q: Look just at the boxes: which data is more spread out – the female or the male?
A: The female data but not by much.

The first thing to notice is that although the median lines show some difference between the two groups the spread of the two groups in fact looks rather similar. If you just compare medians (or means) you might think that men score higher than women on this measure, but if you look at the spread you can see that we need to be a bit more cautious before drawing this conclusion.

Before we draw any such conclusion let's look at each group separately and consider the question of whether they fall into normal distributions.

3.5.2 Histograms – is my data normal?

Biologists and social scientists have it easy. Most of the things they measure fall into a regular pattern; if you're a psychologist planning a reaction time experiment you would expect a few people to be very fast, a few people to be very slow and most people to fall in the middle category; if you're measuring heights, a few people will be very short, most people are of middling height, and a few people are very tall. This pattern is so common across different sciences that it is called a **normal distribution**.

The normal distribution is easiest to understand as a graph. In the picture below (Blakeslee 1914), college students were asked to stand behind a marker post indicating their height. If you study the picture you can see there is 1 individual who is 4'10" (147 cm), 1 individual who is 6'2" tall (188 cm) and, in the middle bunch, 78 individuals between 5'6" and 5'8" (167–172 cm). Today's students will certainly be taller as we have grown as a population, but the pattern, the distribution, will be more or less the same.

This photograph is a kind of human histogram and is more traditionally portrayed in a graph – as you will see on the following page.

The data collected is never entirely neat – we've plotted the histogram of all our responses to the Klingon questionnaire in the histogram on the following page. Looking carefully at this you may be able to see that it is very approximately the smooth bell-shaped curve of a normal distribution. We can use software such as SPSS to calculate how a neat bell curve would fit over this data, and this is shown in the histogram.

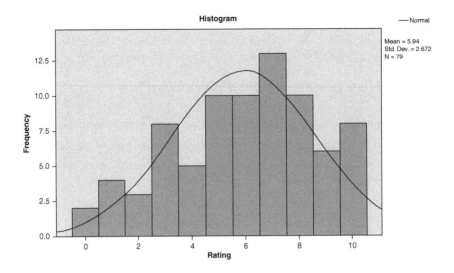

The curve is not a very good fit here. There seems to be a spike of scores at the top end where the curve should be falling. It may be better to split this Klingon survey data by gender and look at the histograms for males and females separately.

Here are the graphs with bell curves added:

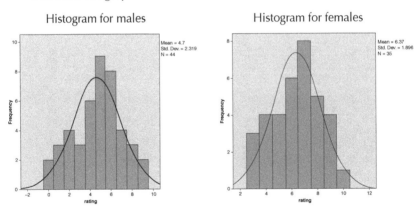

We can now see that both of these look reasonably as though they have normal distributions. In both graphs the histogram falls more or less into the bell-shaped curve. This gives us some confidence that each separate distribution is more or less normal, and this will become important when we consider carrying out statistical testing.

Because of the importance of deciding whether the data is normal it is possible to carry out a statistical test to answer just this question.

3.5.3 *Statistical test for normality*

In some cases just studying your graphs will tell you whether the data is different from normal, but in many cases it may not be clear. There are two statistical tests you can run on your data to give a definitive answer. They are the Kolmogorov-Smirnov (or K-S) test (which is good for bigger data sets) and the Shapiro-Wilk (which can be used where there are fewer than about 50 participants). SPSS provides both of these tests, as do other software packages. The result of the test is a probability that the data is **different from** normal. A very low probability demonstrates that the data is likely to be different from a normal distribution. A higher score shows that it is unlikely that the data differs from a normal distribution. There is a convention that if this probability – called the **significance** score – falls below 0.05 then the data should be treated as different from normal. This idea of significance is discussed further in the glossary.

For our Klingon data we have more than 50 participants so we used the one-sample K-S test.

This gave the following results:

	One-sample K-S sig. value	Conclusion
Female	0.461	Cannot be shown to be different from normal
Male	0.245	Cannot be shown to be different from normal

3.5.4 *Why does it matter whether your data is normal?*

Normality matters in two practical ways:

A. *Measure of central tendency and of spread*

If your data is close enough to a normal distribution you can use the **mean** as the measure of central tendency, and you can use the **standard deviation** as the measure of spread.

If your data is not normal, these two measures may not be as meaningful, and you should consider whether it makes more sense to use the

median, either together with the mean or on its own, as the measure of central tendency and **quartiles** as the measure of spread.

With cases on the borderline, you need to think hard about the different information that is contained in a mean and a median and how this information helps you tell a sensible story about your data. You might choose to quote both. There are no hard and fast rules here – remember that these descriptive statistics are a language to help you describe your data. You need to pick the bits of the language that make most sense in this description. In the Klingon case the mean and standard deviation work for us.

B. The statistical tests you can use

Certain statistical tests (*t*-tests and ANOVAs and some more powerful correlation techniques) need the data to be roughly normal. Such tests are sometimes called **parametric tests**.

If the data is not normal, then you need to use other tests, or **non-parametric tests**.

Q: If you want to perform a statistical test on the Klingon data to compare the ratings awarded by females with the ratings awarded by males, could you use a *t*-test?

A: Yes – the one-sample K-S test showed the data was sufficiently normal.

Q: What if the data for one of the genders was normally distributed, but the data for the other gender was not normally distributed?

A: You could not use a parametric test such as a *t*-test. You would have to use a non-parametric test like the Mann-Whitney U test instead.

Q: Can you perform a non-parametric test on normal data?

A: Yes.

Q: In that case why bother with parametric tests? Why not just use non-parametric tests, because they can work on any data, normal or not?

A: As textual linguistic data rarely falls into normal distributions some linguists very rarely use parametric tests, but where you do have normally distributed data, parametric tests are more powerful than non-parametric ones. A 'powerful' test in this sense is one that is likely to find a result. This means that if you perform a non-parametric test on normal data, it may not find a significant result where a parametric test would find a significant difference so you will have missed an opportunity in your data.

3.6 Drawing statistical conclusions from the data

How to carry out a *t*-test is explained more fully in the chapter on personal pronouns in academic journals, but for completeness of this research story we have carried out the *t*-test on this Klingon data.

The *t*-test result gives a probability that the two samples (of men and women respectively) are drawn from the same population. If this figure is low we can infer that there is a likelihood that they were drawn from different populations – that is to say, the two groups are different from one another on this measure.

The result of the *t*-test on the Klingon data gives a t score of 3.44 with degrees of freedom of 77 and a probability of 0.001.

Conventionally, the result would be written like this:

$$t_{(77)} = 3.44; p > 0.001$$

Degrees of freedom reflects the number of participants in the study. For different tests it is calculated slightly differently, but for a *t*-test it is the number of participants overall, minus the number of groups. The probability figure is very small, representing that there is a 1 in 1000 chance that the two samples are drawn from the same population – on this basis we can feel confident in asserting that it is likely that the groups of men and women appreciate the erotic qualities of Klingon differently.

Our conclusion is therefore that men and women score the erotic quality of Klingon differently, with men judging it to be significantly more erotic than women do!

When you write up this result you would want to reflect back on the literature in your research story (Coupland and Bishop, 2007), which suggested that women were more likely to rate as attractive accents different from their own. Our study suggests that men find Klingon more erotic than women do. There will be plenty to write about in a discussion as to whether these two findings contradict one another and, if so, why this might be.

 ## 3.7 References

Blakeslee, A.F. (1914). Corn and men: the interacting influence of heredity and environment – movements for betterment of men, or corn, or any other living thing, one-sided unless they take both factors into account. *Journal of Heredity* 5 (11), 511–518.

Cheng, W. (2011). *Exploring corpus linguistics: language in action*. London: Routledge.

Coupland, N. and Bishop, H. (2007). Ideologised values for British accents. *Journal of Sociolinguistics* 11 (1), 74–93.

Garrett, P. (2010). *Attitudes to language*. Cambridge: Cambridge University Press.

4 Who speaks Low German with their children?
Visualisation – describing words with pictures

 4.1 The research story

In providing an answer to this question we will look at how you can use visualisation effectively to tell your research story. Our research story for this chapter is based on an ethnographic study of a bilingual village speaking Low German and standard German in northern Germany which was conducted in 2001. Low German is a regional language spoken in northern Germany and parts of the Netherlands, as shown on this map:

Low German is in the process of language shift, which means that it is endangered. Most of its speakers belong to the older generations, and most parents do not raise their children to speak it. This has to do with the fact that Low German carried a stigma of being the language of the uneducated for a long time.

As part of the ethnographic study a survey was conducted in 2001 in order to ascertain the villagers' attitudes towards Low German and to find out more about their linguistic practices. This predominantly qualitative study included a component in which every household in the village was approached and asked to fill in a questionnaire. The village had 520 inhabitants at the time; 125 (24%) of the questionnaires were returned and evaluated.

Two of the questions asked were:

1. Would you actively support the preservation of Low German?

2. Which language do you speak with your children?

The survey revealed an interesting paradox: the general attitude towards Low German was positive, but the vast majority of speakers did not raise their children in Low German (Reershemius 2002: 171). Two contradictory ideologies seemed to be at work: on the one hand, speakers felt that Low German was an important part of their heritage and identity, but, on the other, they still feared their children would be disadvantaged at school if Low German were their first language. Our research story is just one example of many you could come up with. We focus in this chapter on how to visualise quantitative findings. We will discuss different ways to tell the above research story in graphs and tables.

Similar research questions from sociolinguistics might be:

- *Where have Welsh speakers learnt Welsh – at home or in school?*
- *What is the spread of ages in people who speak Breton?*

4.2 The role of visualisation

Visualisation in tables, graphs or charts is a preliminary stage in analysing quantitative data. Doing this allows you to get a feel for what the data might be showing and may prompt you to form some hypotheses about what the data shows. Proving or disproving your hypotheses then requires you to apply statistical tests, as described in other sections.

4.3 Tables

Tables are not often thought of as a form of visualisation, but by designing your tables carefully and thinking about what to present in a table, you can begin to illustrate your research story.

Question:

Look at these tables and ask yourself: how easy is it to see our research story from these figures?

Would you actively support the preservation of Low German?

Age	Yes	Undecided	No	Total
15–30	7	2		9
31–40	15	5		20
41–50	11	2	2	15
51–60	19	2	1	22
Over 60	34			34
Total	86	11	3	100

Which language do you speak with your children?

Age	Low German	Low German and standard German	Standard German	Total
15–30	1	5	2	8
31–40		12	9	21
41–50	2	6	9	17
51–60	5	6	12	23
Over 60	20	6	9	35
Total	28	35	41	104

Answer:

It is probably quite difficult to see the story from these raw figures. You may note:

- There are larger numbers of older people who both support the preservation of Low German and also speak it.

- There are unequal numbers of respondents in the age ranges – there were more older respondents than younger ones.

The second point confounds the issue – perhaps looking at the percentage of responses within each age group will help to make things clearer.

Question:

Look at the tables below and ask yourself: what is your impression of our research story from these figures? Is that impression any different from when you analysed the tables with the raw numbers?

Would you actively support the preservation of Low German?

Age	Yes	Undecided	No	Total
15–30	78%	22%		100%
31–40	75%	25%		100%
41–50	73%	13%	13%	100%
51–60	86%	9%	5%	100%
Over 60	100%			100%
Total	86%	11%	3%	

Which language do you speak with your children?

Age	Low German	Low German and Standard German	Standard German	Total
15–30	13%	63%	25%	100%
31–40	0%	57%	43%	100%
41–50	12%	35%	53%	100%
51–60	22%	26%	52%	100%
Over 60	57%	17%	26%	100%
Total	27%	34%	39%	

Answer:

Things that may be more apparent from these two graphs:

- *Would you actively support the preservation of Low German?*
  - The 'Yes' responses are high across all age groups.
  - The only 'No' responses were from people aged 41–60.

- *Which language do you speak with your children?*
  - The percentage of those over 60 speaking Low German with their children may not seem as high as you might have thought when you looked at Table 4.2.
  - The percentage of younger people speaking both languages with their children seems quite high.

Conclusion:

Tables are not a particularly intuitive way of presenting and reading this numerical data. Raw figures and percentages can give differing impressions. In practice, a table should ideally give both the raw *and* the percentage figures.

4.4 Charts and graphs

4.4.1 Basics

Graphs and charts can be a valuable inclusion in a research paper as they will often be more readable than numbers presented in a table. In our experience, students of linguistics tend to favour pie charts and over-use them. Some students think such charts are objective results and therefore constitute an analysis in themselves. We would like to reiterate here that visualising quantitative data is only one step in the analysis. Therefore, graphs and charts should be accompanied by written explanation, and, as mentioned at the start of this section, ideas that seem apparent through visualisation should be followed up by further analysis.

Visualisations for the survey question: Would you actively support the preservation of Low German?

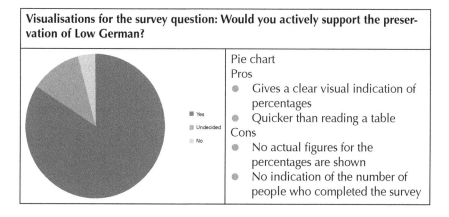

Pie chart
Pros
- Gives a clear visual indication of percentages
- Quicker than reading a table

Cons
- No actual figures for the percentages are shown
- No indication of the number of people who completed the survey

Yes
Undecided
No

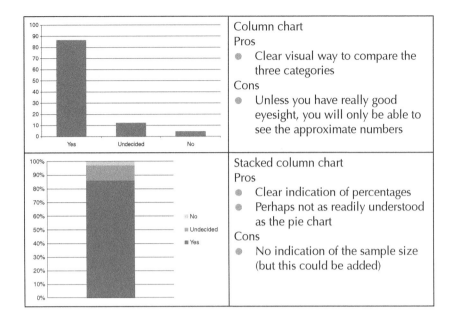

	Column chart Pros ● Clear visual way to compare the three categories Cons ● Unless you have really good eyesight, you will only be able to see the approximate numbers
	Stacked column chart Pros ● Clear indication of percentages ● Perhaps not as readily understood as the pie chart Cons ● No indication of the sample size (but this could be added)

Question:

Which visualisation above represents the data of our research story in the clearest way?

Answer:

While newcomers to quantitative analysis may have a tendency to prefer the pie chart, the column chart may be the clearest option. Note that all the charts above should have labels showing the numbers for each segment or column, as well as the overall sample size.

4.4.2 When things get more complicated

Visualisations by age group for the survey question: Would you actively support the preservation of Low German?

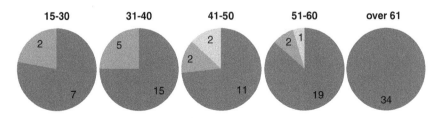

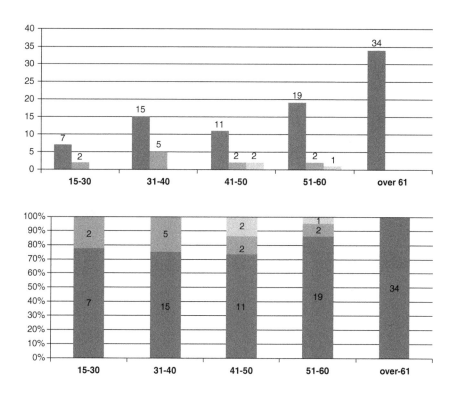

Question:

Which of the above visualisations represents the data of our research story in the clearest way?

Answer:

The third chart – stacked column – is possibly the clearest visualisation and is easy to create in Excel.

The second chart – the column chart – is also a clear representation. However, if there were more than three columns, this could become difficult to read.

Multiple pie charts are rarely a good choice – if you find yourself producing multiple pie charts, stop and think of an alternative. In addition, the ones shown above can be more difficult to produce, take up a lot of space, and need to be arranged carefully to be readable.

Note how the charts above have been given data labels with the numbers in them

4.5 When visualisations mislead

Question:

Study these two column charts, showing responses to the question 'Which language do you speak with your children?' Can you spot the difference? Which graph is more 'honest'?

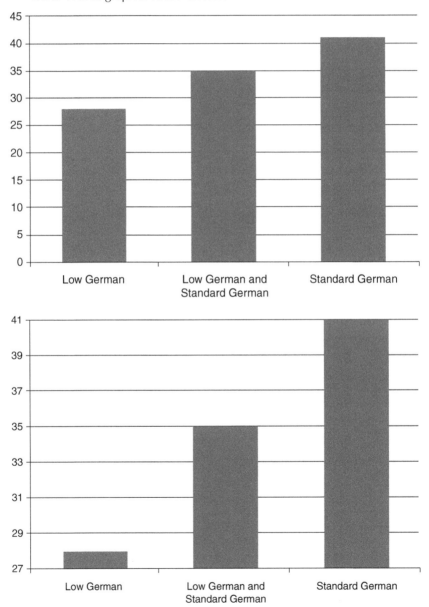

Answer:

Neither graph is dishonest, but you should always check the scale of a graph! Sometimes newspapers will publish graphs with no indication of where the scale starts, and that is more misleading.

 ## 4.6 Boxplot graphs

Boxplot graphs are an ideal visualisation for data that contains *continuous* numbers (see Chapter 1 on types of numbers). You may not be familiar with these graphs because you require a statistical software package to produce them easily. They give a good overview of the descriptive statistics of a data set.

For our boxplot visualisation we will leave the Low German story and look at a different but related data set: the 2004–2006 Welsh Language Use Survey (Welsh Language Board 2008). This survey attracted over 7000 respondents from across Wales and included two questions we will examine: age and competence in Welsh.

Question:

Look at this boxplot graph of age and different levels of ability in Welsh. Do the more competent speakers appear to be older than the speakers at lower levels?

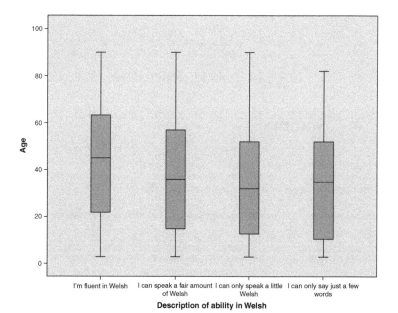

Answer:

It does appear that the group that claims to be fluent was a little older than the other groups. So, from looking at the graph we have an idea, or hypothesis. We do not know if the apparent difference is *significant* or not. We would now need to perform statistical tests in order to prove or disprove that hypothesis. The following chapters explain such tests.

Key to the boxplot:

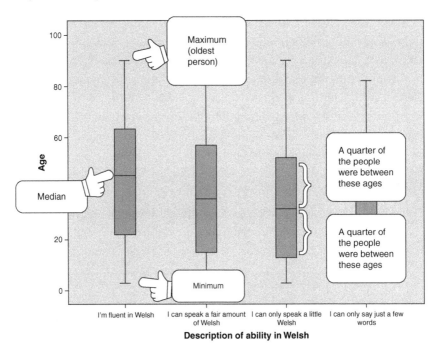

4.7 Summary

1. Visualisation can be in tables, charts or graphs.

2. Visualisation can help you to form hypotheses.

3. Visualisation is a preliminary step to be followed by analysis, for example statistical testing.

4. Tables should indicate percentages as well as raw figures.

5. Graphs and charts are often easier to read than tables.

6. Graphs and charts should include labels showing numbers.

7. Deciding the best chart to use requires some thought.

8. When reading charts created by others, pay attention to where the scale starts or you may be misled.

9. Boxplot graphs are a very effective visualisation you can produce easily using statistical software such as SPSS.

4.8 References

Reershemius, G. (2002). Bilingualismus oder Sprachverlust? Zur Lage und zur aktiven Verwendung des Niederdeutschen in Ostfriesland am Beispiel einer Dorfgemeinschaft. *Zeitschrift für Dialektologie und Linguistik* LXIX (2), 163–181.

Welsh Language Board. (2008). The Welsh language surveys of 2004–2006. Available from: http://doc.ukdataservice.ac.uk/doc/7477/mrdoc/pdf/74 77-methodology-in-english.pdf [Accessed 16 March 2016].

5 Whose English uses more present perfect?

Comparison of two groups where the data is not normally distributed – Mann-Whitney U test

This research study poses the question:

Is use of the present tense more frequent in UK English than in Indian English?

The process of testing this hypothesis illustrates the importance of two concepts that sound very similar but have very different meanings: *normalised* data and *normal* (that is, normally distributed) data.

After tackling our hypothesis, we also ask whether our data might be used for another purpose.

Similar research questions might be:

- *Do students in one language learning class make more plural agreement errors than a different class learning by a different approach?*

- *Do 20–25 year olds use more abbreviations in their online messaging than 26–30 year olds?*

5.1 The research story

There has been increasing interest in the different types of variation that can be found in different Englishes as spoken and written around the world. Early work on world Englishes tended to focus on pronunciation features and local dialect items, but this variation can be seen in syntactic structures too. In their article 'The Present Perfect in World Englishes', Yao and Collins (2012) explore the use of the present perfect form in a variety of genres across different areas around the world where English is spoken. Their conclusion is that varieties of English closest to British English continue in their use of the present perfect form, but the more American-influenced varieties are less likely to use the present perfect.

Responding to this, we decided to collect a corpus of film reviews to explore whether any difference could be found in this respect between the British English newspaper reviews and those from Indian newspapers. Because of the colonial history up through the twentieth century Indian English is typically seen as being closer to British English so any difference that can be found here would be particularly interesting.

5.2 The data

5.2.1 Data collection

We created a small corpus of newspaper articles from two Indian news-papers and two UK newspapers. We extracted the film reviews from each newspaper for the top 20 films in 2012. Within this limited domain, we wanted to see if there was a difference in the frequency of use of the present perfect tense between UK newspapers and Indian newspapers.

5.2.2 Data normalisation

Q: If you want to compare the number of occurrences of a grammatical feature in two texts, should those two texts be the same length?

A: The texts do not have to be exactly the same length, but you have to take account of differing lengths by **normalising** the data. You cannot compare the raw number of occurrences, but you can compare the relative frequency, for example the number of occurrences per 1000 words. If you do that, you have normalised the data.

In each review, we counted the number of occurrences of the present per-fect tense and, from that, worked out how many times the tense was used per 1000 words in that review.

Here is a table of frequency of use of the present perfect tense in each review. These figures are not the number of occurrences but, instead, the number of occurrences per 1000 words.

Film title	Times (London)	The Guardian	Times of India	The Indian Express
bridesmaids	0.31	0.81		0.00
captain-america	0.41	0.55	0.00	0.35
cars-2	0.20	0.43	0.00	0.22
fast-five	0.30	0.47	0.27	0.56
hangover	0.16	0.67	0.23	0.00
harry-potter	0.62	0.37	0.00	0.65
kung-fu-panda	0.45	0.00	0.26	0.00
mission-impossible	0.70	0.00	0.22	0.29
pirates	0.49	0.69	0.27	0.21
planet-of-the-apes	0.58	0.47	0.17	
puss-in-boots	0.31	0.36	0.45	0.19
rio	0.32	0.74	0.00	1.00
sherlock	0.78	0.42	0.16	0.18
smurfs	0.46	0.00	0.00	0.75
super-8	0.32	0.20		0.00
the-help	0.00	1.09	0.33	1.52
thor	0.89	0.21	0.00	0.45
transformers	0.17	0.61	0.22	0.54
twilight	0.60	0.00	0.00	0.77
x-men	0.33	0.00	0.52	0.00

Note: Blank cells indicate the film was not reviewed in that paper.

5.3 Descriptive statistics

We would like to compare UK newspapers with Indian newspapers. So we put the data for each review into SPSS. A few lines of the data table are given below to show the format:

	Review	Film	Newspaper	Nationality	Present perfect per 1000
31	64	2	Indian Express	India	3.50
32	73	17	Indian Express	India	4.46
33	92	18	Indian Express	India	5.44
34	94	4	Indian Express	India	5.65
35	101	6	Indian Express	India	6.46
Etc.					

5.3.1 Averages and spread of data

	N	Mean	Median	Standard deviation
UK	40	4.12	4.18	2.69
India	37	2.92	2.19	3.30

Q: Why does $N = 40$ for the UK but $N = 37$ for India?
A: Because not all 20 films were reviewed by both of the Indian newspapers.

Q: On average, in which country is the frequency of use of the present perfect higher?
A: The UK.

Q: In which country is the spread of frequency the greatest?
A: India.

5.3.2 Is the data normally distributed?

Let's repeat: do not confuse the notion of **normalised data** with the notion of **normally distributed data**! These notions are quite different! Just because you have normalised your data does not mean your data has a normal distribution!

Let's look at histograms first.

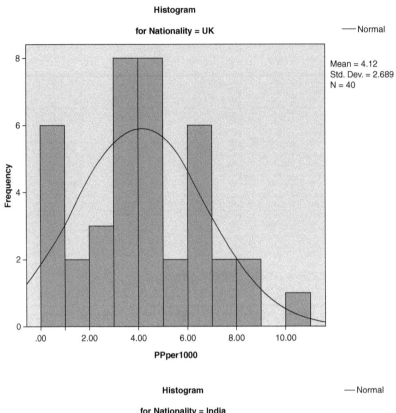

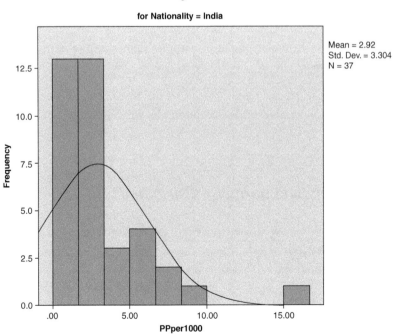

Q: Does the UK data look normally distributed?

A: More or less but the zero scores are worrying.

Q: Does the Indian data look normally distributed?

A: The issue with the zero scores is even worse here. I've even tested it with a one-sample K-S test; although the UK data is on the borderline, the Indian data is shown to be definitely not normal ($p < 0.001$).

Q: The UK sample is doubtful and the Indian sample is definitely not normal – what shall I do?

A: If you were wanting to use the *t*-test to ask whether there was a statistical difference between the two groups you would need to understand better how much the *t*-test relied on the data being normally distributed. The answer for beginners is that you should use a *t*-test only if the data is normal and so in this case must look for a different test to use (e.g. one based on comparative ranking of the data, such as the Mann-Whitney U test).

It is possible to give a more advanced answer that a *t*-test can be used on some types of non-normal data if the sample size is large enough (e.g. more than 100 data points). Unless you are willing to do some more advanced reading (and thinking) the safest route would be to use a test that doesn't have an assumption of normality.

5.3.3 Describing the data with pictures

The standard boxplot graph is based on the median and the quartiles and so is perfectly appropriate to use with this non-normal data.

Q: Does the spread of results look very different?

A: No. The size of the two boxes – showing where 50% of the cases are – looks similar.

Q: Does that data look to be normally distributed?

A: In both cases the median is in the middle of the box, so it does look as though it might be normal, but the problem with the zero scores shows on the boxplots too. The Indian box is squished right up to the zero line.

Q: Have I just got unlucky here?

A: No. You're a linguist, and you need to come to expect this – textual data is rarely normal.

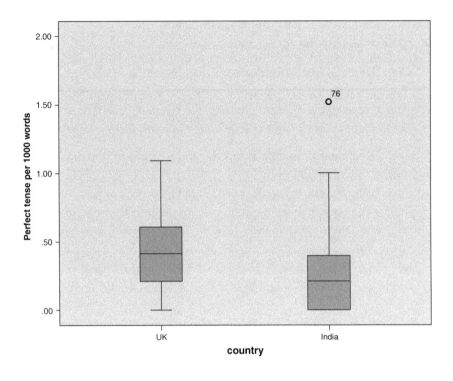

5.3.4 Linguists and non-normal data

If you are a linguist working as a social scientist – for example if you are researching language attitudes, language testing or some aspects of language teaching – then your data may create something like a normal distribution. The Klingon example in Chapter 2 was close to normal. Any well-designed language competence test or assessment should aim to produce a normal distribution of results.

If you are a linguist working on text analysis – for example looking at the frequency of a particular grammatical feature in texts – your data is unlikely to fall into anything like a normal distribution. Analysis of textual data very rarely falls into a normal distribution. Even considering the simplest corpus statistic of word frequency distribution you can easily see that the graph looks nothing like the bell curve of our normal distributions:

In this graph, ordered by frequency, we can see function words like *the, of* and *and* which are very high frequency; then, whatever the size of

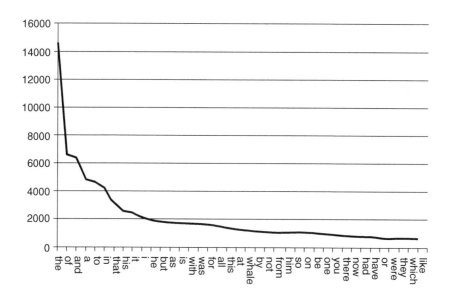

the corpus, the frequency rapidly falls until about half the words in any corpus are only used very rarely.

This curve very roughly approximates what is called a log-normal distribution, and this shape of distribution occurs in many types of language investigation. If you are studying error counts for language learners, the use of dialect items in a particular sociolinguistic group or variant pronunciation features in a particular group, in each case you will find a few common high-frequency features and then a long list of rarer possibilities. Although you can use more advanced statistical techniques to transform the patterns of data and treat it as if it were normal, it is best and easiest to recognise that this is not normally distributed data and so you need to make sure you treat it accordingly.

Linguists are also interested in the rarer things in life. We like to study the coinage of new words, or, as with the Black Country corpus project, discussed in a later chapter of this book, it can be interesting to study a few individuals who speak an interesting language variety. In these cases you may be dealing with very small groups of data points.

If you have a study like this where your counts are low, with each feature being used just once or twice, then your data is never going to fall into a normal distribution. This does not mean that you cannot or should not quantify your data. You just need to use tests that do not need normal data.

5.3.5 Drawing inferential conclusions from non-normal data

If your data is not normal do not despair! There is a whole set of statistical tests, sometimes referred to as non-parametric tests, which deal with non-normal data. Some of these tests work by treating the data as rank ordered so that the shape of the distribution doesn't matter so much.

A non-parametric test suitable for comparison of two groups is called the Mann-Whitney U test; this ranks all the scores in the analysis and then examines whether one group in general ranks higher than the other.

A Mann-Whitney U test was run on the above data and showed that UK film reviews ranked as using the present perfect tense more than Indian film reviews, with mean ranks of 33 and 47 respectively.

The Mann-Whitney U test showed that this ranking demonstrated a significant difference between the two groups of reviews: Mann-Whitney $U_{(n=80)} = 517$; $p = 0.006$.

This is interesting with regard to our research story. Initially we hypothesised that Indian English might be close to British English, but with regard to the use of the present perfect tense in this genre we can show that there is a difference. In writing up the discussion we might focus on exploring further contrasts, for example with American English and/or Chinese English. We might look at other genres than newspaper film reviews, or we might look to quantify other linguistic features.

5.4 A follow-on research story? Identifying words that might merit further investigation

This sub-section – an adjunct to the main focus of this chapter – looks at how, after answering one research question, you may wish to identify ways in which you could exploit your data further.

Having completed the study of the present perfect tense, we now ask ourselves whether our film review corpus may contain interesting lexical items which we would want to investigate further using *qualitative* methods. We can thus use *quantitative* corpus techniques to assist us in identifying words that will be interesting in a more *qualitative* analysis. It is important to remember that quantitative and qualitative methods are not alternatives where you have to choose just one approach – some of the richest answers to research questions use a combination of quantitative and qualitative techniques to explore data.

We can use corpus tools to help with identifying interesting words – either by looking at words that occur most *frequently* or words that are most *key*.

Let's try looking at the most frequent words first.

5.4.1 What are the most frequent words?

Here are the top 20 entries in the word list for the film review corpus as a whole – including both UK and Indian reviews:

Rank	Frequency	Word
1	2617	the
2	1283	and
3	1274	a
4	1088	of
5	854	to
6	788	in
7	675	is
8	586	s
9	405	it
10	404	with
11	374	that
12	353	as
13	322	for
14	303	his
15	271	film
16	258	this
17	253	on
18	251	but
19	223	he
20	216	who

Q: What does this tell us about the words used in this corpus?
A: Not very much. Apart from the noun *film*, the list is of functional words that you would find in any collection of texts.

5.4.2 What are the most interesting words?

If a researcher is looking to find words in a corpus that merit further investigation, a frequency list may not be the most efficient way of identifying
the important words. Instead, they might look at *key* words. Key words are
words whose frequency in a text or corpus is statistically significant when
compared to the frequency in a reference corpus (Scott 1997). That is to
say, a word is considered key if it occurs more often (or less often) than
expected compared to some baseline corpus.

The keyness of words is calculated by statistical tests that do not
assume that data is normally distributed. Two such tests are *chi square*
and *log likelihood*. Chi square is explained in Chapter 6 of this book. Log
likelihood is described by Rayson (2008), and we will not explain it further
here – we mention it merely to show that two different types of test might
be used to achieve the same thing, each with its own advantages.

Let's compare the whole of the film review corpus against a general-
purpose corpus. We will use the LOB (Lancaster-Oslo/Bergen) corpus,
which is a collection of general British English compiled in the 1970s. Put-
ting aside the question of how suitable this is as a reference corpus, let's
make the comparison. Standard corpus software such as Wordsmith Tools or
AntConc will assist you, whether by calculating keyness scores for you or by
producing word lists so that you can calculate keyness statistics for yourself.

Here are the top 20 key words, excluding proper nouns and the titles
of the films that were reviewed:

Keyness using chi square				Keyness using log likelihood			
Rank	Frequency	Keyness	Keyword	Rank	Frequency	Keyness	Keyword
1	271	3685.676	film	1	271	1151.951	film
2	107	2456.022	movie	2	107	653.752	movie
3	59	1312.329	mins	3	59	349.822	mins
4	45	1074.882	pg	4	45	289.288	pg
5	36	788.230	movies	5	76	218.310	length
6	27	644.929	doesn	6	36	210.524	movies
7	61	553.554	director	7	61	203.728	director
8	76	537.740	length	8	27	173.573	doesn
9	27	535.754	franchise	9	27	146.246	franchise
10	20	453.074	sequel	10	36	137.236	hero
11	36	407.957	hero	11	31	129.154	screen

12	31	407.754	screen	12	44	128.924	captain
13	28	385.487	comedy	13	20	120.614	sequel
14	16	382.180	vampire	14	28	119.900	comedy
15	28	376.126	comic	15	33	118.368	fun
16	17	359.752	guys	16	28	118.138	comic
17	33	337.535	fun	17	216	110.112	who
18	19	335.858	animation	18	58	109.306	section
19	19	335.858	starring	19	16	102.858	vampire
20	14	334.408	cert	20	51	99.577	action

You will see from these figures that the two methods of calculating keyness give very similar results.

Let's try looking at the figures for the UK newspapers and for the Indian newspapers. We will compare each to the LOB corpus, and we will use chi square.

UK reviews				Indian reviews			
Rank	Fre-quency	Keyness	Keyword	Rank	Fre-quency	Keyness	Keyword
1	72	2805.321	movie	1	119	2556.514	film
2	152	2716.416	film	2	35	1775.896	movie
3	59	2271.101	mins	3	18	1021.807	doesn
4	45	1855.729	pg	4	13	636.114	guys
5	27	996.701	movies	5	22	602.632	super
6	26	612.478	comedy	6	9	510.904	superhero
7	19	612.403	franchise	7	23	499.757	hero
8	14	577.338	cert	8	18	465.252	drama
9	18	547.755	starring	9	12	446.172	animation
10	14	536.984	sequel	10	15	410.885	rating
11	41	510.251	director	11	7	397.370	vampire
12	11	453.623	superhero	12	9	378.691	movies
13	22	431.889	screen	13	20	372.824	fun
14	15	412.265	voiced	14	7	345.951	quotient
15	19	372.995	comic	15	34	320.011	length
16	9	371.146	cameo	16	7	305.962	monkey
17	9	371.146	doesn	17	6	290.233	sequel
18	9	371.146	vampire	18	7	273.975	pirates
19	42	333.182	length	19	8	273.349	franchise
20	8	329.907	prequel	20	11	241.531	furious

Once you have identified lists of key words there are many questions that can arise for the researcher:

Q: Looking at these lists, which – if any – words might you want to investigate further?

Q: How would you investigate these words?

Q: Are there specific corpus analysis techniques you might use? (Hint: You might start by looking at key words in context (KWIC) to spot typical collocates.)

Q: Are there broader quantitative or qualitative techniques that might help you explore the use of these words across British and Indian English?

Q: How do these analyses more broadly inform our exploration of world Englishes in our film review corpus?

In this example we have looked at using keyness to identify frequency. However, it can also be used to identify infrequency, to see which words are less common in a specific collection of texts than in a reference collection.

For further guidance on how to use keyness statistics in corpus linguistics, see Cheng (2011).

5.5 Summary

1. Some statistical tests – *parametric tests* such as a *t*-test – require data to be *normal*.

2. If your data is not normal, you need to use a *non-parametric* test, such as a Mann-Whitney U test.

3. If your data is normal, you can use the *mean* as the average. If it is not normal, you should use the *median* as the average.

4. You can see whether a data set *appears* to be normal by looking at histograms and boxplot graphs.

5. You can *test* whether data is normal using a Kolmogorov-Smirnov (K-S) test or a Shapiro-Wilk test.

6. Linguists working on text analysis will often encounter data sets that are not normal.

7. Do not mix up the concept of *normal data* (that is, data with a normal distribution) with the concept of *normalising* data (e.g. using occurrences of the present perfect tense *per 1000 words* instead of per film review).

8. Corpus analysis tools can calculate the *keyness* of words using statistical tests – either *chi square* or *log likelihood*.

9. Combining quantitative and qualitative methods can lead to the richest linguistic research questions and answers.

5.6 References

Cheng, W. (2011). *Exploring corpus linguistics: language in action*. London: Routledge.

Rayson, P. (2008). From key words to key semantic domains. *International Journal of Corpus Linguistics* 13, 519–549.

Scott, M. (1997). PC analysis of key words – and key key words. *System* 25, 233–245.

Yao, X. and Collins, P. (2012). The present perfect in world Englishes. *World Englishes* 31, 386–403. doi:10.1111/j.1467-971X.2012.01756.x

6

Is there a difference in the way 'ing' is pronounced by people from Birmingham and the Black Country?

Testing for difference using chi square

This research question compares *two* groups in relation to *one* topic. It looks at how often a *nominal* (a.k.a. categorical) variable occurs. There is a small number of data samples, so it is unlikely the data will have a normal distribution.

Other similar research questions are:

- *Do men take more turns in pub/dinner party/cafe conversations than women?*
- *Do first year student essays have a simpler clause structure than third year student essays?*

 ## 6.1 The research story

The research story for this chapter is based upon an ethnographic study of the accents and dialects associated with the West Midlands region of the UK. The project investigated the extent to which locally based performers such as actors, comedians, folk musicians, poets and storytellers drew upon the accent and dialect associated with their locality in local, live performance events.

Sociolinguists had predicted that linguistic variety in English would eventually die out, through a process known as dialect levelling. This was due to a number of factors, such as that increasing numbers of people were becoming literate in standard English and that standard English is the accent and dialect heard and read the most in print, film, TV and other media. Added to this was the fact that traditional, unskilled blue collar manual labour, which required very little literacy, has virtually disappeared, in many urban regions of the UK especially. Such jobs have by and large been replaced with more white collar ones that demand that the workforce is literate. Sociolinguistic research has also shown that speaking with a recognisable accent and dialect are correlated with social class. It is clear that dialect levelling is occurring, particularly in relation to lexis and morphosyntax. However, a great deal of variation can still be heard in relation to phonological features associated with accent and pronunciation. The main aim of the project was thus to test the theory that people were deliberately drawing upon linguistic variation to mark an identity linked to place, rather than to social class.

The main aim of the project, turned into a research question, was: **Do performers deliberately and self-consciously draw upon a set of identified, regional variables to mark an identity linked to place?**

To answer this question, a qualitative ethnographic study was undertaken between 2009 and 2013, involving audio-recording live performance events and interviews with the performers. These recordings were then transcribed, and variation marked using the International Phonetic Alphabet (IPA). Although the data for the project was collected ethnographically, the length and number of sound recordings meant that quantitative analysis could be undertaken in relation to identifying the number of occurrences, or frequency, of the variables identified. This is important because the more often a variable occurs, the more it can be said to be a salient, that is, noticeable and recognisable, feature of the accent or dialect under investigation.

This main research question led to a number of subsidiary research questions, of which one was to identify a set of lexical, morphosyntactic and phonological variables related to contemporary use of linguistic variation in the West Midlands region of the UK. In relation to the data discussed in this chapter, the specific regions under investigation are those of the city of Birmingham and a neighbouring region known as the Black Country.

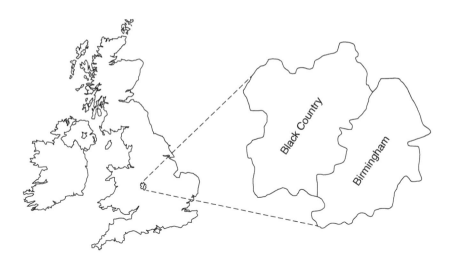

This chapter draws upon a sub-set of data that allows us to look at how two subjects – one from Birmingham, one from the Black Country – pronounce 'ing'.

Q: What are the distinctive phonological variables associated with Birmingham and the Black Country?

A: One distinctive feature of both regions that has been identified in previous research is *nasality*. This is the production of sound issued through the nose, known in phonetic (speech sound) description as *velar nasal plus*. In English this feature relates to the pronunciation of 'ng', for example in words such as *sing*, *fling* or *hang*.

Q: How many ways are there of pronouncing 'ing'?

A: In Birmingham and the Black Country accents there are three variants:

1. The **velar nasal** sound, represented in IPA as [ŋ]. It can occur more than once in a word, for example in *singing*, which in IPA is [sɪŋɪŋ].

2. **G-dropping**, represented in IPA as [n]. For example, pronouncing *speaking* as [spiːkɪn], and represented in writing as *speakin'*.

3. The **velar nasal plus**, found in some English accents, such as those of the West Midlands region of the UK. Where this occurs, the velar nasal [ŋ] is 'over-articulated', being immediately followed by the sound [g]. For example, in 'Birmingham the segment -ing- is pronounced [ɪŋg], making the pronunciation more like 'Birming-gam' or [bɜːmɪŋgəm] in IPA.

The research question discussed in this chapter is:

Is there a difference between the Black Country and Birmingham in the choice of these three variants?

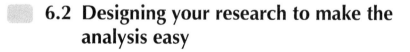

6.2 Designing your research to make the analysis easy

The nature of this question is a *between group* analysis. For between group analyses you need to make sure that the two groups are completely separate from one another. The number of people who take part in your research is known as a *sample* or *sampling*. In sociolinguistic research, this means that your groups can be distinguished in terms of non-linguistic variables such as age, ethnicity and gender or, in the case of this project, in relation to locality and having lived in either Birmingham or the Black Country for most of their lives.

6.2.1 The sample

In designing your data collection in relation to investigating a linguistic feature of pronunciation, you need to make sure that the participants from whom you obtain your spoken data were born and/or have lived in the region being researched for the majority of their lives. You will thus want to exclude participants who have a mixed linguistic history. To ensure this, you can give each participant in your research a brief questionnaire to capture key biographical information (known as biodata), including information relating to where your participants have lived in a particular region and for how long. You could also include information about where their parents are from. Other biodata categories in relation to the data discussed here include information about participants' age, gender, where they went to school and/or college or university, and their occupation/s.

For the example used in this chapter, there is *one* participant in each group, making a total of *two* participants. The two participants were both male comedians, one in his late 50s and the other in his mid-20s at the time of the recordings, and both had been born and had lived in the region for most of their lives, the first in the Black Country and the second in Birmingham.

6.3 The data

The data drawn upon in this example is taken from transcripts of two interviews given by each of two performers, one born and bred in Birmingham and the other in the Black Country, both of whom talk about their performances. The data is thus frequency data – a count of occurrences rather than a score. For this kind of data, a chi square analysis is the best one to use.

6.3.1 Describing the data with words

This experiment uses two groups drawn from separate populations. The measured outcome is the degree of nasality in pronouncing the velar nasal plus sound. Three variants of the pronunciation of 'ing' have been identified: [ɪŋ], [ɪn] and [ɪŋg]. The measure is taken from the number of times each of the three variants of the velar nasal plus occurs in the transcriptions. As discussed above, this is important because the more frequently a variant is used, the more it can be judged to be a characteristic feature of the accent under investigation.

When you are comparing two groups your graph needs to show the spread or *distribution* of judgements for each group but together on just one graph.

6.3.2 Describing the data with pictures

First, you will need to enter your data into a spreadsheet:

Total number of occurrences of [ɪŋ], [ɪn] and [ɪŋg]

	A	C	D	E
1		**Birmingham**	**Black Country**	**Total**
2	**Duration**	00:30:00	00:45:00	01:15:00
3	[ɪŋ]	53	49	102
4	[ɪn]	28	97	125
5	[ɪŋg]	7	12	19

An immediate issue here is that of *normalisation*. The Black Country interview is 45 minutes long, and the Birmingham interview is 30 minutes.

They are thus unequal in length. The Black Country interview is one third longer than the Birmingham one. We therefore have to normalise the length of the Black Country interview for the purposes of comparison. This involves dividing all the Black Country counts by two thirds, to get the table below:

Normalised occurrences of [ŋ], [ɪn] and [ɪŋg]

	A	C	D
1		**Birmingham**	**Black Country**
2	**Normalised duration**	**00:30:00**	**00:30:00**
3	**[ŋ]**	53	33
4	**[ɪn]**	28	64
5	**[ɪŋg]**	7	8

From the spreadsheet you can create a *visualisation* (see previous chapter), which for this data is best presented as a column chart:

In this chart you can see that the Birmingham performer prefers the [ŋ] variant, and the Black Country performer the [ɪn] variant.

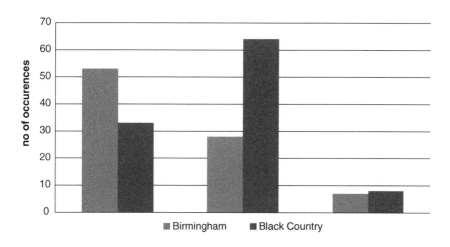

Such a visualisation gives an idea of the overall picture in relation to the three variants and the frequency of use. However, if you wish to find out whether or not the differences are significant, then you need to undertake a statistical analysis, which in this case is chi square.

6.3.3 Describing the data with numbers

To calculate a chi square, we compare the *observed* frequencies with the *expected* frequencies.

Q. Observed? Expected? What does that mean?
A. Read on, and follow these steps.

Step 1: Take the data you recorded. This is the observed data.

	A	C	D
1		Birmingham	Black Country
2	Normalised duration	00:30:00	00:30:00
3	[ŋ]	53	33
4	[ɪn]	28	64
5	[ɪŋg]	7	8

Step 2: Calculate the totals.

	A	C	D	E
1		Birmingham	Black Country	Total
2	Normalised duration	00:30:00	00:30:00	
3	[ŋ]	53	33	86
4	[ɪn]	28	64	92
5	[ɪŋg]	7	8	15
6	Total	88	105	193

Step 3: Delete the observed data, but leave the totals.

	A	C	D	E
1		Birmingham	Black Country	Total
2	Normalised duration	00:30:00	00:30:00	
3	[ŋ]			86
4	[ɪn]			92
5	[ɪŋg]			15
6	Total	88	105	193

Note: If you are performing step 3 in a spreadsheet, the formulae that calculate the totals need to be replaced with the raw figures.

Step 4a: Calculate the *expected* figure for cell C3.

	A	C	D	E
1		Birmingham	Black Country	Total
2	Normalised duration	00:30:00	00:30:00	
3	[ŋ]	39.2		86
4	[ɪn]			92
5	[ɪŋg]			15
6	Total	88	105	193

Here is the formula for cell C3 worded in three ways:
=C8*E3/E8
=88 times 86 divided by 193
=column total times row total divided by overall total

Step 4b: Calculate the *expected* figures for the other cells.

	A	C	D	E
1		Birmingham	Black Country	Total
2	Normalised duration	00:30:00	00:30:00	
3	[ŋ]	39.2	46.8	86
4	[ɪn]	41.9	50.1	92
5	[ɪŋg]	6.8	8.2	15
6	Total	87.9	105.1	193

Q: So what next?

A: Let's look at the numbers side by side and see if there are any interesting differences between what was observed and what was expected.

		Observed			Expected	
		Birming-ham	Black Country		Birming-ham	Black Country
[ŋ]		53	33		39.2	46.8
[ɪn]		28	64		41.9	50.1
[ɪŋg]		7	8		6.8	8.2

Q: OK, I see that for [ŋ] Birmingham is higher than expected, and the Black Country is lower. Then, for [ɪn], Birmingham is lower than expected, and the Black Country is higher. Isn't that what we saw in the graph anyway?

A: It is indeed.

Q: So why bother with what was observed vs what was expected?

A: We have shown you this simply so you understand the notions of *observed* and *expected* figures, and therefore have a little insight into how chi square works.

6.4 Answering the question with chi square analysis

From the column chart and the observed and expected figures, we have a *hypothesis*:

- Birmingham and Black Country accents pronounce 'ing' differently.

If we have a hypothesis, there is a matching *null hypothesis:*

- There is no difference in the ways Birmingham and Black Country accents pronounce 'ing'.

A *null hypothesis* is the hypothesis that there is no significant difference between the populations specified and that your predicted hypothesis is not upheld.

To confirm our hypothesis, we want statistical evidence, so we perform a chi square test on the data. To do this, we used the software SPSS.

6.4.1 The chi square test

The following data was entered into SPSS.

SampleNumber	Region	Pronunciation	Frequency
1	Black Country	[ɪŋ]	33
2	Black Country	[ɪn]	64
3	Black Country	[ɪŋg]	8
4	Birmingham	[ɪŋ]	53
5	Birmingham	[ɪn]	28
6	Birmingham	[ɪŋg]	7

The first row shows the SPSS variable names. For each of the four variables, before entering the number as well as the name, we told SPSS the type of data that variable would hold.

We had to tell SPSS what kind of data each column held:

- SampleNumber, Region and Pronunciation were *nominal*.
- Frequency was *scale*. *Scale* is SPSS's name for a *continuous* number.

There are many books and websites explaining how to use SPSS, with varying levels of detail and ease of access for the novice user.

A chi square was calculated with the following result:

- $X^2 = 83$
- Degrees of freedom = 5
- $p < 0.001$

The probability figure tells us there is less than a 1 in 1000 chance that the null hypothesis is true. So we reject the null hypothesis. This is a complicated way of saying our hypothesis is supported and we can assert that the Birmingham and Black Country performers pronounce 'ing' differently.

6.4.2 *Writing up your result*

Conventionally, the results of the chi square would be reported as:

> A chi square analysis showed a significant difference between the Birmingham and Black Country performers in their pronunciation of 'ing' ($X^2_{(5)} = 83$; $p < 0.001$).

6.5 Summary

1. A chi square analysis used in this way compares *two* groups in relation to *one* topic.
2. The two groups are completely **separate** from one another.

3. The **variable** being investigated has two or more **categories**, with no intrinsic ordering of the categories in question.

4. The data relates to frequency – a count of **occurrence** rather than a score.

5. A chi square works on **observed** vs **expected** frequency.

6. There is a set way to write up the test results.

Do letter writers tend to use nouns and verbs together?
Scatterplots and correlation of linear data

This research question involves comparing the relationship between the relative frequencies of two parts-of-speech measured across a series of texts, to see if the frequency of one part-of-speech rises or falls with the frequency of the other part-of-speech. Given this type of problem, the most common approach is to use scatterplots to visualise the relationship between the two variables and a Pearson's correlation coefficient measure to test the strength of the relationship between the two variables.

Other research questions that are similar to this are:

- *Is the relative frequency of adjectives and adverbs related?*

- *Is the frequency of pronoun usage related to author age?*

- *Does the use of coordinating conjunctions tend to rise with the speaking rate?*

7.1 The research story

The English language contains many different parts-of-speech, including nouns, verbs, adjectives, adverbs, prepositions and pronouns. Although each part-of-speech has a different function, an interesting question is whether or not different parts-of-speech pattern together, tending to occur frequently in the same texts. In particular, this study looks at whether or not nouns and verbs – two of the most common parts-of-speech in any language – tend to occur together in a corpus of American letters to the editor.

There are various possible results that we could find. First, it may be the case that texts that have a lot of nouns also tend to have a lot of verbs and that texts that have very few nouns tend to have very few verbs. This is called a *positive correlation*. Note that this possibility could also be stated equivalently the other way around: that is, that texts that have a lot of verbs tend to have a lot of nouns and that texts that have very few verbs tend to have very few verbs. Second, it may be the case that texts that have a lot of nouns tend to have very few verbs and that texts that have very few nouns tend to have a lot of verbs (or vice versa). This is called a *negative correlation*. Third, it may be the case that there is no relationship at all between the two variables, that is, that knowing whether a text has many or very few nouns or verbs does not allow us to predict how frequent the other part-of-speech will be. Finally, various other more complex patterns are also possible. We might also hypothesise that a negative correlation might be most likely, given that these two types of part-of-speech are doing very different things (i.e. describing entities vs actions), and therefore a text with a large number of nouns will arguably have less space for a large number of verbs and vice versa.

By measuring the frequency of these parts-of-speech across a corpus of letters to the editor and by then measuring the correlation between these frequencies, it is possible to verify which of these types of relationships holds.

The research question discussed in this chapter, then, is:

What is the relationship between the relative frequency of nouns and verbs in American letters to the editor?

7.2 Designing your research to make the analysis easy

To conduct this analysis you need a corpus of texts. In this case, we will look at letters to the editor.

7.2.1 The sample

The complete corpus from which the data for this study was drawn is a 36 million word corpus of American letters to the editor published in major American daily city newspapers from 2000 to 2013. In total, the corpus contains data for 240 different cities. This study, however, is based on data from four of these cities, chosen essentially at random. The main analysis will focus on the data from Cleveland, Ohio, but in order to test the stability of the pattern, we will also consider data from Birmingham, Alabama; Boston, Massachusetts; and Tulsa, Oklahoma. In total, the corpus contains 302 letters for Cleveland, 185 letters for Birmingham, 660 letters for Boston, and 527 letters for Tulsa. Because the letters from each city will be analysed separately, it doesn't matter that the number of letters varies.

Although this analysis focuses on letters to the editor from four American cities, this study could easily be repeated for other registers of the English language, and using other parts-of-speech or really any type of linguistic forms (e.g. affixes, words, grammatical constructions). In general, it is good to have as many texts as possible when doing this type of correlational research, as this will help to ensure that the results are reliable, but you do not necessarily need hundreds of texts, as we are using here. As few as thirty or so texts would be sufficient to run this type of analysis. The texts themselves can also be different lengths, since we will normalise them (see below), but it is important that the texts are long enough to reasonably contain at least a few examples of the features under analysis. Letters to the editor are usually a couple hundred words long, which gives us plenty of chances to observe verbs and nouns, which are very frequent parts-of-speech, as you would imagine.

7.3 The data

Once you have assembled a corpus it will be necessary to count the nouns and verbs in each of the texts. This could all be done by hand, especially if you are working with a small corpus, but a better solution is to automatically identify the part-of-speech of each word in your corpus using a *part-of-speech tagger*. Various free taggers are available online or for download. Just search for 'part-of-speech tagger' online. Once you've found a tagger you like, you just need to paste your raw text into the tagger, and it will output a text where each word has been annotated with a part-of-speech tag. For example, if you entered the sentence 'The old dog barked softly', a tagger might return 'The_DT old_JJ dog_NN barked_VBD softly_RB', where 'DT' stands for *determiner*, 'JJ' stands for *adjective*, 'NN' stands for *singular common noun*, 'VBD' stands for *past tense verb*, and 'RB' stands for *adverb*. Be careful, though: the *tag sets* used by different taggers vary. Check the documentation associated with the tagger for more information.

After the corpus of texts has been tagged, the frequency of a part-of-speech can be easily counted using any basic corpus analysis tool or even many text editors, all of which can be freely downloaded online. In most tag sets noun tags begin with an 'N', while verb tags begin with a 'V', as you would expect, although most taggers will make additional distinctions, such as using the tag 'VBD' for past tense verbs. In this case, we just want to count all nouns and all verbs, so we do this by counting the number of words that contain the character sequences '_N' and '_V' in each text in order to obtain the frequency of nouns and verbs in general. This process was then repeated for each text in the corpus.

In addition to counting the total number of nouns and verbs in each text, it is also necessary to count the total number of words in each text, so that we can normalise our noun and verb counts. We need to do this because our texts are of different lengths. For example, if one letter has 50 total words in it and another has 250 total words in it, then obviously the second text will have more nouns and verbs than the first text. So comparing the frequencies of nouns and verbs in these two texts will not tell us much. In order to get comparable data we need to normalise our frequency counts. This means turning *raw frequencies* into *relative frequencies*, which can then be compared across texts of different lengths. Basically, we do this by dividing the frequency counts for nouns and verbs by the total number of words in that text and then multiplying this value by a constant. It does not matter which constant you use, but usually corpus linguists use a round number, like 100, 1000, or 1,000,000. Once you pick your constant you can then start saying things like nouns occur this many times per hundred, thousand or million words. Just make sure you are consistent across all of your texts, so if you use 100 for the first text, you need to use 100 for all subsequent calculations so that the values are comparable. In this case, we will use a normalising constant of 100 because both nouns and verbs are very common parts-of-speech, so they tend to occur multiple times per 100 words. Once you do that, instead of saying that nouns, for example, occur in the first text 67 times out of 152 words and in the second text 43 times out of 98 words, which is not really comparable (in fact, it looks as though nouns are more common in the first text), we can say that nouns occur ($100 \times 33 \div 152 =$) 22 times per 100 words in the first text and ($100 \times 26 \div 95 =$) 27 times per 100 words in the second text, which allows us to directly compare the relative frequency of nouns in both texts, and in this case see that nouns are actually slightly more common in the second text. Note that if we had used 1000 words as the normalising constant, the numbers would have increased to 217 times per 1000 words and 274 times per 1000 words, but the result – that nouns are more common in the second text – would remain the same.

As it is collected, this data should be entered into a spreadsheet, with the texts as rows (*cases*) and the parts-of-speech as columns (*variables*). For example, this is what the first few rows of the spreadsheet for the Cleveland data looks like, where we have rounded the value to the nearest whole number (in total, there are 302 rows in this spreadsheet, one for each of the letters in the corpus):

Letter	Nouns	Verbs
1	22	14
2	23	20
3	28	15
4	25	12
5	22	14

7.3.1 Describing the data with pictures

When looking at the relationship between the values of two quantitative variables measured over a series of cases, such as the relative frequencies of two parts of speech measured over a series of texts, the most standard and useful graph is called a *scatterplot*. Basically, each case (e.g. text) is assigned a pair of coordinates based on the values of each of the two variables (e.g. relative frequency of nouns and verbs in that text). Each case can then be plotted in a two-dimensional graph based on the values of these two variables, with one variable plotted on the x-axis and one variable plotted on the y-axis, sort of like a map. In this way a scatterplot makes it possible to visualise whether and how the two variables are related, for example if both variables tend to rise in value together, or if one variable rises as the other falls, or if there is no obvious relationship between the two variables. Other more complex patterns might be visible as well. Assuming there is a relationship between the two variables, with one variable rising or falling as the other rises, a scatterplot also allows you to assess whether this relationship is linear (i.e. following a straight line) or non-linear (i.e. following a curved line). This in turn can affect which correlation coefficient you use to measure the strength of this relationship (see below).

The scatterplot for the relative frequency of nouns vs verbs for the 302 letters to the editor in our corpus from Cleveland, Ohio, is presented below. Each dot in the scatterplot represents one of the 302 letters (although note that some dots overlap). The position of the dot on the horizontal x-axis depends on the number of nouns in the letter, which ranges from a minimum of 0 to a maximum 62 times, while the position of the dot on the vertical y-axis depends on the number of verbs in the letter, which ranges from a minimum of 0 to a maximum of 33. Note that the order of the two axes could be reversed. It would not make a difference. The scatterplots show that there is quite a clear relationship between the relative frequency of nouns and verbs in letters to the editor from Cleveland, Ohio, specifically with texts that contain lots of nouns tending to contain relatively few verbs and with texts that contain a lot of verbs tending to contain relatively few nouns. You can see this because most dots on the far right hand side of the graph, which means they are texts with lots of nouns, tend to be relatively low, which means they are texts with relatively few verbs, whereas most dots on the far left hand side of the graph, which means they are texts with relatively few nouns, tend to be relatively high, which means they are texts with lots of verbs. Because nouns and verbs show opposite patterns, with one part-of-speech rising as the other falls and vice versa, we say they are *indirectly related* to each other. Had they risen and fallen together, we would have said they are *directly related* to each other. It is also important to note that although the scatterplot is sort of fat in the middle and skinnier at the ends, the pattern looks to be roughly linear, in the sense that the downward trend follows a pretty straight line, rather than being curved (e.g. starting off steeper and then gradually levelling off).

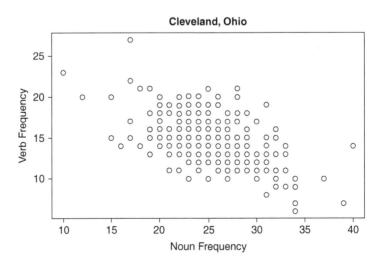

For comparison, and to see just how consistent this pattern is, we repeated this same analysis for the corpora of letters to the editor from Boston, Birmingham, and Tulsa. We can see a remarkably similar pattern across all three of these graphs, with the relative frequency of nouns clearly decreasing as the relative frequency of verbs increases. This pattern is therefore clearly quite robust: it would appear that in general in American letters to the editor, the use of nouns is inversely proportional to the use of verbs.

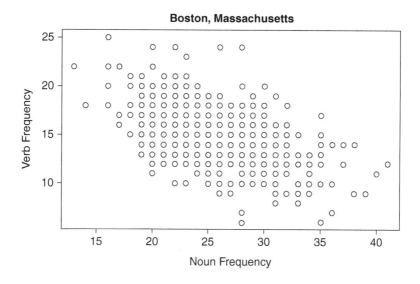

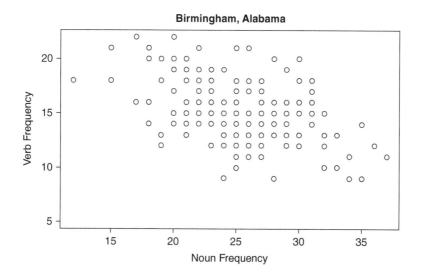

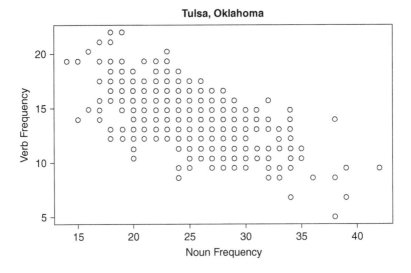

Tulsa, Oklahoma

7.4 Answering the question using a Pearson's correlation analysis

It is always very important to visualise your results. In fact, in most cases it is probably more important to visualise your results than to conduct statistical analysis. In part, this is because it lets you see general patterns and make sure there are no problems or weird things happening with your data, but it is also often necessary to visualise your results in order to decide how to proceed with your statistical analysis. For example, in this case, we can see not only that trends exist in our data but that they are roughly linear. This means that if we want to measure the strength of the relationship between the relative frequencies of nouns and verbs in our corpus we can use a linear correlation coefficient, *specifically Pearson's correlation coefficient*, which is one of the most basic and common measures you can use. If the data was non-linear (e.g. had a curving pattern), then another correlation coefficient, such as *Spearman's correlation coefficient*, would have been a better choice.

Although we have already seen that a relationship exists between the relative frequencies of nouns and verbs in our data based on the scatterplots, the great advantage of calculating a correlation coefficient is that it will allow us to quantify just how strong this relationship is. It will also allow us to compare the strength of the relationship across the different cities, which might be very interesting. In particular, a Pearson's correlation coefficient, which is generally represented by the symbol r, can range between −1 and +1, where −1 represents a perfect negative correlation (i.e. one variable rises steadily as the other falls), +1 represents a perfect positive correlation (i.e. both variables rise steadily together), and 0 represents no correlation at all (i.e. the rise in one variable has no effect on the value of the other variable). In this case, given that we have seen that nouns and verbs are inversely related in all of our data sets, we know that we'll get negative correlations for all of our cities. The question is how strong these negative correlations will be. In addition to comparing the correlation coefficients across our different cities, to see where this relationship is strongest, we can also interpret each correlation coefficient individually following general *rules of thumb*. In particular, in the social sciences and humanities, Pearson's correlation coefficients between ±0.7 and ±1 are generally considered to be *strong*, those between ±0.4 and ±0.6 are generally considered to be *moderate*, and anything lower is considered to be weak.

Because it is such a basic statistic, it is very simple to calculate a Pearson's correlation coefficient using any spreadsheet or statistical software package. You just need to identify the two variables you are analysing, which will be represented by a series of paired numbers. For example, given the table above, you could just select the two columns and then ask the program you are using to calculate a Pearson's correlation coefficient for each of your data sets. Doing that with our data we get the following correlation coefficients:

Cleveland: $r = -0.5466523$

Boston: $r = -0.4762975$

Birmingham: $r = -0.5289402$

Tulsa: $r = -0.5628217$

Based on these results, we can conclude that there is a moderate negative correlation between the relative frequencies of nouns and verbs in letters to the editor from all four of these American cities. Given that these results are relatively stable, it seems likely that this pattern would hold in general for American letters to the editor, although we might want to look at a few more cities to be sure, especially in the western United States, which is excluded from this sample. We might also see if the same relationship holds in other English-speaking countries. Furthermore, we can also compare the strength of this relationship across the different cities in our corpus. In this case, we can see that the relationship is strongest in Tulsa and weakest in Boston. It would be interesting to follow up this research by checking whether there is any overall regional dialect pattern in the strength of this relationship across a large number of American cities. For example, perhaps the relationship is stronger in the Midwest or the Southeast.

Does the use of pronouns differ between two academic disciplines?
Using *t*-tests to compare two groups

Other research questions similar to the one above are:

- *Do women use more hedges in tweets than men?*
- *Do higher status employees use fewer markers of politeness in e-mails than lower status employees?*

 ## 8.1 The research story

Do different academic subjects have distinctive patterns of pronoun use?
One question that students often ask when writing assignments is: should I avoid personal pronouns? There is a sense that personal pronoun use is somewhat non-academic and that to write successfully in an academic register one needs to carefully ration any use of pronouns. Pronouns are a closed class set of features, which means that (in contrast to open class items) we do not generally create new pronouns over time (notwithstanding some very long-term diachronic changes in the use of English pronouns), and this means that we have a very well-defined set of items, an ideal situation for a *corpus-based analysis*.

The research question discussed in this chapter, then, is:

Does pronoun use vary significantly across different academic disciplines?

8.2 Designing your research to make the analysis easy

The nature of this question is again a between group analysis. For between group analyses you need to make sure that the two groups are completely separate from one another. The number of people or texts that provide the data for your study is the *sample*. Collections of naturally occurring data chosen to represent a particular variety of language are often called *corpora*, and the analysis of these has become very prevalent in applied linguistics. The sample here can again be ordered in any way (since the order of the texts is not relevant to the research question), but for simplicity it is sensible to have an ordering principle of some sort; the one chosen here is again to organise the texts alphabetically, using the surname of the first author as the name for the paper.

8.2.1 The sample

The data collection for this investigation requires two representative samples of different academic disciplines. These samples should take into account issues of genre and register in order to prevent variables associated with these from constituting confounding factors in the analysis of the frequency and distribution of pronouns. We thus need to focus on one particular text type (in this case, the academic research article) and to ensure that the research articles are typical of the academic discipline they are supposed to represent. We chose the *Journal of Modern History* to represent the discipline of history and *Genome Research* to represent the discipline of genetics since each of these has been ranked as among the top ten international research journals in their respective fields in recent years. One complicating factor when studying academic English is the international nature of the discourse community. In a previous section we used a representative sample from Birmingham and the Black Country where the age and personal history of the participants was taken into account to ensure that the sample was consistent. When we are studying academic English this is much more difficult to achieve, for a number of reasons. Academics publishing in international journals tend to be from a wide variety of national backgrounds and often tend to have moved around geographically – almost certainly regionally and nationally but very often internationally as well. A typical issue of an academic journal will contain articles by academics from a number of countries where English may or may not be the first language, or even an official language, of the population. Finally, academic journal articles are often written by a number of authors, and in the case of scientific journal articles there may be a very large list of named authors (sometimes as many as 50 or even over 100 researchers), and the actual role of each of these in writing the article will not usually be made clear, notwithstanding the convention that the first, last and second named authors are understood to have had the most significant roles in producing the research. The solution to this seemingly intractable problem is to remember that we are interested in studying a particular variety of English, produced by a specific discourse community, rather than a clearly defined set of native speakers or speakers from a specific geographical origin. As such, the *Journal of Modern History* and the journal *Genome Research* represent the discourse communities of academic history and genetics, and we can be confident that writing that is published in these journals is typical of academic writing in these disciplines.

8.3 The data

The data for this example is two sets of research articles from two contrasting academic disciplines, history and genetics. For each journal 30 articles have been selected, and the total number of pronouns in each article has been counted. Pronouns are relatively frequent, and counts of pronouns will produce variation between texts on a continuous scale. Because of this the differences between groups may fall into approximately normal distributions. For comparison between two groups with data on a continuous scale a *t*-test can be a powerful analysis even with a fairly small number of texts and so is appropriate for this problem.

Twenty-eight pronouns were counted for each text. These are described as word forms and are *I, me, mine, myself, you, your, yours, yourself, he, him, his, himself, she, her, hers, herself, it, its, itself, we, us, our, ourselves, yourselves, they, them, their, themselves*. The occurrences of each of these will then be added together to give the *total number of pronouns* in each text.

A section of the table for the *Journal of Modern History* is shown as entered into a spreadsheet:

	Total tokens	Total pronouns	Pronouns per 1000 words
1	17,570	436	24.82
2	15,976	288	18.03
3	17,854	575	32.21
4	13,650	338	24.76
5	17,616	705	40.02
6	12,752	334	26.19
7	14,802	324	21.89
8	15,185	459	30.23
9	12,896	394	30.55
10	14,583	326	22.35

8.3.1 Normalisation

The issue of *normalisation* is important here, and it is worth reflecting on how often this needs to be taken into account, particularly when working with naturally occurring language data. Since the length of the texts cannot be constrained by the researcher, there is inevitably variation. If we look at the table above we can see the *token* count for each text. This is the total number of words in each text, and we can see that there is considerable variation here, even just in the first ten texts from the sample. The longest text (text 3) contains 17,854 tokens, whilst the shortest (text 6) contains 12,752. This is a considerable difference (text 3 is roughly a third longer than text 6), and of course this will affect the total number of pronouns present in each text. We therefore need to normalise the length of the texts. This involves dividing the total number of pronouns found by the total number of tokens in the text. For ease of presentation we can then multiply this by a figure divisible by ten. In this case, we have multiplied by 1000, and this gives us the numbers in the fourth column D: the total number of pronouns per 1000 words.

8.3.2 Describing the data with words

The measured outcome is the number of personal pronouns in each text, normalised per 1000 words.

The *t*-test allows us to assess whether the two samples are drawn from a single population or represent counts drawn from two separate populations.

For our question we can assess whether pronoun use is consistent within a single genre of academic writing or whether it varies enough across the two journals to suggest there are two sub-genres of academic writing in our data. One result from the *t*-test will be the probability value, and we will be able to read this as a probability that the data is drawn from a single population.

8.3.3 Describing the data with pictures

A boxplot visualisation gives an initial view of the frequency distribution of pronouns across the two journal samples:

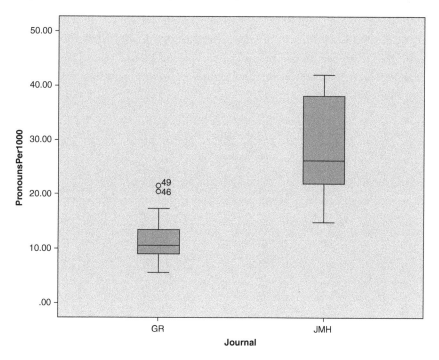

The first point we note is that, indeed, it looks as though there is a clear difference between the two distributions. The two boxes representing half the cases in each group show no overlap at all, and there is very little overlap between the top quartile for *Genome Research* and the bottom quartile for the *Journal of Modern History*. This is highly suggestive that we will be able to demonstrate a difference between the two groups using a *t*-test or other statistical test.

There may, however, still be a problem in carrying out a *t*-test, as to do so the data must fall within certain assumptions. Further examining the boxplot is the first stage in assessing whether the assumptions for a *t*-test can be met.

8.3.4 The normality of the distributions

For a *t*-test to be reliable, both sets of data – the pronoun distribution for *Genome Research* and for the *Journal of Modern History* – should be *normally distributed*. To assess this using the boxplots we need to look at the symmetry of the box and whisker plots and the thick black line in the middle of the box, which represents the median figure. If the data is normally distributed this black line should be close to the centre of the box for each journal.

This doesn't look to be the case, and we can use further visualisations and statistical tests of normality to see whether the distribution of pronouns is close enough to being normal to be acceptable. These are further described in Chapter 3. In this case, the histograms show that although the pronoun distribution for the journal *Genome Research* is roughly normal, the pronoun distribution for the *Journal of Modern History* looks more problematic.

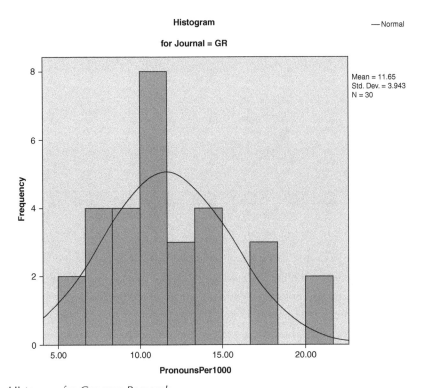

Histogram for *Genome Research*

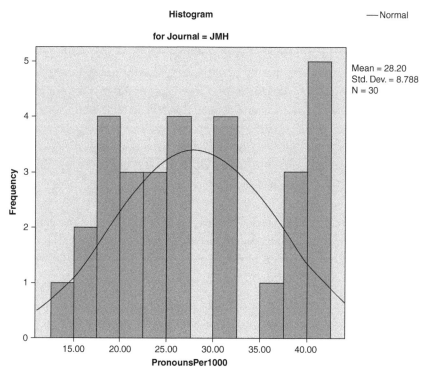

Histogram for the *Journal of Modern History*

These histograms lead us to use the Kolmogorov-Smirnov (K-S) test to determine whether the distributions are statistically different from normal; the results were that neither distribution could be shown to differ from normal (*Genome Research* one-sample K-S test$_{(30)}$ = 0.15; $p > 0.05$ | *Journal of Modern History* one-sample K-S test$_{(30)}$ = 0.14; $p > 0.05$). In this research we have 60 articles we are comparing, which is a fairly good number, and the literature suggests that the *t*-test is fairly robust under these circumstances; so, unlike for the question above where we looked at the use of the present perfect tense in the film review corpora, we've decided to carry on. Even though we know the distributions are not perfectly normal the results from the K-S test suggest the problem is not too severe and give us sufficient confidence to proceed.

8.3.5 *Equality of variance*

Returning to the boxplots, they also show that the samples don't have similar *variances*. This can be assessed by looking at the shape of the two boxes. As we can clearly see, the box for *Genome Research* is much shorter and fatter than the box for the *Journal of Modern History*. This is less important as an assumption for the *t*-test as there are versions of the test that don't assume equality of variance. A useful test here is Levene's test for the equality of variances, and the result of this test for our data is Levene's statistic$_{(1,58)}$ = 25.9; $p < 0.001$. This tells us that there is a significant difference in the variance between our two sets of data.

From our visualisations, therefore, we have been led to draw some preliminary conclusions and to conduct some preliminary quantitative data analysis. The points so far are:

1. That given the general lack of overlap of the boxplots, the two genres of academic writing as represented by these articles in these two journals appear to use pronouns in different ways (with the *Journal of Modern History* using more pronouns);

2. That the boxplots suggest the data samples are not perfectly normal, but further visualisation and the K-S test result suggest this should not prevent us from carrying out a *t*-test;

3. That the boxplots and the Levene result suggest that there is a difference in variance between the two samples, and we should be careful to use the appropriate *t*-test result.

8.3.6 Describing the data with numbers

Having examined our data visually, we have discovered that it is approximately normally distributed. With this information we now know that it will be useful to calculate the mean and standard deviation for the samples of articles from each of the two journals. If the data were not normally distributed it might make more sense to use other descriptive statistics such as the median score.

The table following shows these results that reinforce with numbers our interpretation of the boxplots, that there are more pronouns in the *Journal of Modern History* but also that in this journal there is more variation in the use of pronouns. The larger standard deviation indicates that the distribution is more spread out, that some writers use a lot of pronouns but that other writers use relatively few pronouns.

We can also use these figures to help us make a guess at what we might find with the *t*-test. The difference in the mean number of pronouns between the two groups is about 17 pronouns per 1000 words (mean for *Journal of Modern History* = 28.2; mean for *Genome Research* = 11.7; 28.2 − 11.7 = 16.5). The bigger standard deviation for the two groups is about 9 (*Journal of Modern History* = 8.79), and this is much less than the mean difference, which seems to indicate a degree of difference between the two groups.

Group statistics for *Journal of Modern History* and *Genome Research* (pronouns per 1000 tokens)

Journal	Mean	Standard deviation
Journal of Modern History	28.2	8.79
Genome Research	11.7	3.94

8.4 Answering the question with a *t*-test

We are now ready to carry out the *t*-test; from our visualisations and pre-liminary analyses we already have a pretty strong idea of the answer we are going to get. Finally, we can proceed with our *t*-test. We carried out the *t*-test using SPSS and got the following set of results. Other packages give the results in a different layout, but whatever you use, you need to read the results carefully.

From our preliminary testing we noted that the variance between our two samples is different. In the table above we can see that SPSS provides two rows of results, one entitled 'Equal variances assumed' and one entitled 'Equal variances not assumed'. This gives us two alternative sets of results for the *t*-test depending on whether we have equal variances in our samples or not. Since we have established that we do **not** have equal variances we need to read our results from the bottom line.

In the box labelled 'Sig. (two-tailed)' we see the significance figure for our *t*-test. This gives a significance figure of 0.000. It is important to recognise that this figure is misleading and should not be quoted. It is a probability figure and can be read as the probability that the two samples are drawn from the same population. That is to say, it is the probability that the two samples of articles are inseparable and drawn from the one over-arching genre we are calling academic writing. It is clearly nonsense to

Independent samples test

		Levene's test for equality of variances		t-test for equality of means				Standard error difference	95% confidence interval of the difference	
		F	Sig.	t	df	Sig. (two-tailed)	Mean difference		Lower	Upper
Pronouns per 1000 words	Equal variances assumed	25.955	0.000	9.409	58.000	0.000	16.50007	1.80858	13.27559	20.52455
	Equal variances not assumed			9.409	40.223	0.000	16.50007	1.87556	13.09182	20.70832

say that this is a zero probability, and, in fact, this is just a rounding error. From SPSS we can get the significance figure to more decimal places (e.g. 0.0001362), which SPSS has rounded to 0.000. The crucial figure here is 0.05. If the figure for significance is below 0.05 we will be satisfied that this is a significant result. Conventionally, then, we write that there is a significance value of less than 0.001, written as '$p < 0.001$'. This is because the true figure is somewhere between 0.001 and 0.0001362. It is not zero.

Another key figure for us in our set of t-test results is of course the one labelled 't'. If we read this off for the bottom row we see a figure of 9.409. Finally, in order to describe our t-test result with numbers we need a third figure, that labelled 'df'. This is the degrees of freedom, and if we again read this from the bottom row we see that we have a figure of 40.223.

8.4.1 Writing up your result

Conventionally, the result of the t-test is reported as follows:

The use of pronouns in the *Journal of Modern History* was significantly higher than the use in *Genome Research* ($t_{(40.2)}$ = 9.409; $p < 0.001$).

Here, then, we have our result: there is indeed a statistically significant difference in the frequency of pronouns in the *Journal of Modern History* and *Genome Research*. Note that this structure contains each of the three crucial figures that we read from the bottom line of our t-test results. We can see the t-test value of 9.409, the significance figure ($p < 0.001$) and the degrees of freedom (40.2). Note that these are written in this set order with *t* followed by the figure for the degrees of freedom (in brackets and in subscript), the *equals* sign, the t-test value, a semicolon and then, finally, the significance figure. When you present your t-test results you should report the result in precisely this way, including all of these elements, presented in exactly the way that they are here.

 ## 8.5 Summary

1. A t-test compares *two* groups in relation to *one* topic.
2. The two groups are completely **separate** from one another.

3. The **variable** being investigated should comprise continuous data that falls into a roughly normal distribution.

4. It is possible to run a *t*-test **where the variance between the two groups is significantly different**, but under these circumstances we need to read the result from the line **'Equal variances not assumed'**.

5. The **probability figure** can be read as **the probability that the two groups come from one population**.

6. This means that for a **significant result** we are looking for a **very low probability figure** (less than 0.05), **not a high figure**! This is because a **low probability** means that it is **not likely** that the two groups come from the same population.

Do different academic subjects have distinctive patterns of pronoun use?

Comparison between three or more groups – one-way ANOVA

Other research questions similar to the one above are:

- *Do teenagers, people in their 20s and people in their 30s write different length Facebook updates?*

 ## 9.1 The research story

In the previous section we examined whether there was a difference in pronoun use between two academic disciplines as represented by articles in the *Journal of Modern History* and the journal *Genome Research*. We explored this question using a series of visualisations and finally a *t*-test. As with many questions, restricting the question to a comparison between just two groups may not be enough. Many questions we may wish to ask involve three or more groups, and in these cases we need to extend our analytic method.

The research question discussed in this chapter, then, is the same as in the previous section, but we add in one further journal, the philosophy journal *Mind*.

Does pronoun use vary significantly across different academic disciplines?

9.2 Designing your research to make the analysis easy

The nature of this question is again a comparison between groups with three separate groups. As with *t*-tests, it is important that the groups are completely separate from one another.

9.2.1 The sample

In the previous section we chose to examine articles from the *Journal of Modern History* to represent the discipline of history and *Genome Research* to represent the discipline of genetics since each of these has been ranked as among the top ten international research journals in their respective fields in recent years. In this new question we have added the philosophy journal *Mind*, which is considered a good journal in the discipline of philosophy. Our expectation is that philosophy will have a different convention again for academic writing and that this will be reflected in the use of personal pronouns.

9.3 The data

The data for this example is therefore three sets of research articles from three academic disciplines: history, genetics and philosophy. The same 30 articles were used from the *Journal of Modern History* and *Genome Research*, and to this we've added 30 articles from *Mind*. As before, the same 28 pronouns were counted for each text. These are *I, me, mine, myself, you, your, yours, yourself, he, him, his, himself, she, her, hers, herself, it, its, itself, we, us, our, ourselves, yourselves, they, them, their, themselves*. The occurrences of each of these were added together to give the *total number of pronouns* in each text. As for the *t*-test, the data was normalised (per 1000 words), and the table below shows a section of the data table for all three journals. You will notice that after the counts have been normalised you will get results to a number of decimal places. We've rounded this data to two decimal places. You may want to read the previous section for the discussion of why we have normalised the data.

In the table you will also notice that the numbers for *Mind*, even for just the first seven articles for each journal, look considerably higher than for the other two journals. From this briefest snapshot of the data we are already thinking that the philosophers writing in *Mind* use more pronouns than the historians and geneticists of the other two journals.

As with *t*-tests, ANOVA requires the data to fall into roughly normal distributions, and so the process of analysis will be parallel to that carried out previously.

Section of table showing the normalised count of personal pronouns per 1000 words in 30 articles from the *Journal of Modern History*, *Genome Research* and *Mind*

Journal of Modern History	Genome Research	Mind
24.82	13.53	35.62
18.03	16.80	39.36
32.21	7.20	47.76
24.76	9.01	38.29
40.02	7.73	23.78
26.19	13.25	43.68

9.3.1 Describing the data with words

The measured outcome is the number of personal pronouns in each text normalised per 1000 words.

The ANOVA allows us to assess whether the two samples are drawn from a single population or represent counts drawn from three or more separate populations. For our question we can assess whether pronoun use is consistent within a single genre of academic writing or whether it varies enough across the three journals to suggest there are two sub-genres of academic writing in our data. One difference from the *t*-test is that it is possible that two of the journals are within the same genre but that the other journal is distinct.

The ANOVA result will give us an overall probability that the data are drawn from a single population, but, as we will see, we will want to carry out some follow-up, or post hoc, tests to establish whether there are three separate sub-genres or only two.

9.3.2 Describing the data with pictures

The boxplots visualisation is also very useful for ANOVA analyses and gives an initial view of the data.

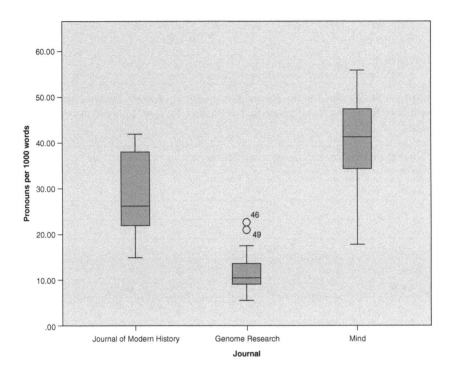

The first point we note is that, indeed, it appears that there is a clear difference between the three distributions. The boxes do not overlap substantially, but there is some overlap between the boxes for the *Journal of Modern History* and *Mind*.

Assumptions for an ANOVA

To carry out a simple one-way ANOVA, the different samples must be independent of one another, and the data must be of a certain type.

- The distribution of each sample must fall into a normal distribution.
- The data across samples should have roughly equal variance.
- There should be an even number of cases in each group.

ANOVA is fairly robust, which means you can get away with breaking one or even two of these assumptions, but to be safest with your analysis you should try to meet all three.

Normality of the distributions

From the boxplot we can visually assess the normality of the distribution. For the new distribution representing the articles from the journal *Mind* we can see that the boxplot does suggest the data is normal. Statistical testing using a one-sample Kolmogorov-Smirnov test confirms this.

Equality of variance across distributions

Thinking about the equality of variance across the groups (which is often referred to as the *homogeneity of variance*) we can see that the three boxes on the plot are of very different sizes. This suggests the variance is different across the three distributions. Using a Levene's test for equality of variance we can confirm this observation (Levene statistic$_{(2,87)}$ = 10.7; $p < 0.001$), suggesting that there is a significant difference in variance across the three groups.

From the observed difference in variance will not stop us from carrying out the ANOVA, however, as we have met two of the three assumptions as described above.

From our visualisations our preliminary conclusions are:

1. That given the general lack of overlap of the boxplots, the three genres of academic writing as represented by these articles appear to use pronouns in different ways: writers in *Mind* appear to use the most pronouns, writers in the *Journal of Modern History* use fewer pronouns, and writers in *Genome Research* use the fewest of all;

2. That the boxplots suggest the data samples are not perfectly normal, but further visualisation and the Kolmogorov-Smirnov test result suggest this should not prevent us from carrying out the ANOVA;

3. That the boxplots and the Levene result suggest that there is a difference in variance between the samples, and we can also see that there is the most variance in *Mind* and the *Journal of Modern History*, with some writers using many pronouns and others using few.

9.3.3 Describing the data with numbers

As before, once we have assured ourselves that the data is roughly normal, it makes sense to calculate the means and standard deviations of each sample; these are represented in the following table.

Group statistics for *Journal of Modern History* Mind and *Genome Research*: pronouns per 1000 tokens

Journal	Mean	Standard deviation
Journal of Modern History	28.2	8.78
Genome Research	11.7	3.94
Mind	39.8	9.20

Studying this table, we should try to work out what result the ANOVA will produce. *Genome Research*, with the fewest pronouns, has on average about 17 pronouns per 1000 words fewer than the *Journal for Modern History*, which in turn has about 11 pronouns fewer than *Mind*. As the largest standard deviation between groups is about 9, this suggests that we will be able to find differences between the samples.

9.4 Answering the question with an ANOVA

At this stage you might be tempted to carry out a series of *t*-tests comparing each journal with each of the others. You should never do this. Carrying out statistical tests is all about probability; each test you run is making a throw of the dice, and if you carry out more tests than you need to, the likelihood increases that you will get an answer which you cannot rely on.

ANOVA helps in two ways. First, it provides a test of difference over all of the samples. Second, it provides a statistically safe way to carry out a number of pairwise comparisons. These are called 'post hoc tests'.

The main result of running the ANOVA on our data tells us that the articles from the three journals do show different pronoun use. The formal result is expressed as $F(2,89) = 101.4; p < 0.001$. This can be read as saying that there is less than a 1 in a 1000 chance that all three samples belong to the same population. From this statistical result, though, we cannot say whether each journal is different from the others or explain why we have this statistical result. We may be content to explain the result using our boxplots and descriptive statistics, but it can also be useful to carry out post hoc tests.

9.4.1 Post hoc tests

One of the easiest post hoc comparisons to understand is a Bonferroni post hoc test. This carries out a similar comparison to a *t*-test but accounts for the statistical risk of multiple comparisons.

In some software that you may use to carry out a Bonferroni comparison, the results table can be confusing as it contains all possible comparisons, including duplicates. Thus, Table 9.3 shows a line comparing *Mind* with *Genome Research* and then on a separate line compares *Genome Research* with *Mind*. It also shows the significance values to be 0.000. This just means less than 0.001.

Here is a slightly edited output from SPSS:

Bonferroni	Journal	Journal	Mean difference	Standard error	Significance
	Journal of Modern History	Genome Research	16.54700	1.98680	0.000
		Mind	−11.60667	1.98680	0.000
	Genome Research	Journal of Modern History	−16.54700	1.98680	0.000
		Mind	−28.15367	1.98680	0.000
	Mind	Journal of Modern History	11.60667	1.98680	0.000
		Genome Research	28.15367	1.98680	0.000

You'll need to look at any data output table carefully and need report only two results. You could write it up like this: 'A post hoc Bonferroni comparison was carried out and showed that *Genome Research* had significantly lower pronoun use than the *Journal of Modern History* (mean difference = 16.54; $p < 0.001$) and also that the *Journal of Modern History* had significantly lower pronoun use than *Mind* (mean difference = 11.6; $p < 0.001$).

9.5 Discussion

When you come to write up your investigation you will of course want to assess whether the statistically significant differences you've found in the numbers represent real differences in the world. Whilst we need to be cautious about over-interpreting the results, in this case the results do seem to reflect very real differences between the styles of the three journals, and perhaps these stylistic differences represent wider differences between genres of each discipline.

Asking and answering quantitative questions
Conclusions

What we have tried to demonstrate through providing these worked examples is that investigating language using quantitative methods is an engaging research process that can give rise to interesting conclusions. Any statistical testing is not simply a final optional step in your research project to provide a single, discrete answer to a narrowly focused question – although of course statistical testing can provide that. Rather, taking a quantitative approach is a designed process that allows for a rich exploration of a linguistic issue and the data you might collect to explore that issue.

In the series of questions and answers, we've introduced a number of visual and statistical approaches, including statistical tests. We hope that you will read through the various questions and answers and find one that is a bit like the problem you are investigating; then you will be able to follow through the steps using your own problem and your own data. Hopefully you've learnt the basic steps for all the projects as suggested at the beginning of Part 2. To recap, these are as follows:

1. Read the literature to develop a research story.

2. Design your study to collect the numerical data.

3. Collect the data.

4. Describe and explore your quantitative data with numbers.

5. Describe and explore your quantitative data with pictures.

6. Draw statistical conclusions from the data using inferential tests.

7. Relate these statistical conclusions back to the research story you developed from the literature.

The methods covered through the questions and answers are of course not the only methods and tests available, and if you have different or more complex problems you will have to find out about different methods and tests. Further, we also hope that by using Part 2 and this book more generally you will have learnt some of the vocabulary you'll need to research, read and understand statistical textbooks that deal with more complex techniques or simply different techniques than those covered here.

10.1 How to ruin your research project (and how to succeed with it)

How to ruin your research project	How to succeed with your research project
Ignore everything you've learnt in the course of your studies and just make up a question. You've got such a good idea for a question that you needn't do any reading or think about what you've studied. Above all, don't make any reference to the research literature when deciding your research question – you're aiming for originality, right?	**A good research project requires reading.** Think about your reading and writing in linguistics to determine your research question. You need to demonstrate a good understanding of the research literature and to show how the research question arises from that literature.
Just do the same study as you did last year and maybe collect slightly different data. That'd be the easy thing to do, after all – you've already got your introduction partly written from the assignment. You wrote it, so it's not plagiarism, right? Even better, that published paper you read, well, you could redo that study. . . with less data. . . and less analysis. That'd do the trick.	**A good research project requires a good research question.** Look at different studies which you've read about and be inspired by them, but don't try to reproduce them – you've probably not got the time and the resources. If you got a good mark on a previous project, you might choose to treat that as a related study (or even a pilot for a dissertation length project), but ask yourself what are you going to add and how you are going to improve it and make it more interesting and different. You will be most motivated if you ask a question where you really want to know the answer – of course replication has a role in scientific advances, but it's not as interesting as finding out something you didn't know before.

How to ruin your research project	How to succeed with your research project
Data analysis involves thinking a bit about the data as you write it up. And pie charts. Lots and lots of pie charts.	**A good research project requires good data analysis.** A good data analysis requires thought and time. Plan your data analysis, and note down and justify every decision you make. Your decision processes as to how you are going to analyse the data are part of the research project, and you need to think through (and report) these processes before you can start reporting your findings. **A really good research project may include a variety of different ways of looking at your data.** You may want to include some quantitative and some qualitative analysis. This is likely to produce a richer answer to your research question (but only if you have explained and justified what it is you are doing, and pull it all together in your write-up). Visualisations can help, but think hard about how and why you are including them. Tables, graphs and charts should be labelled, explained and integrated into the text.
Everyone knows that the best writing is done between 11:30 pm and 4:00 am (which is why the pubs close when they do). This is the natural order of things and allows you a few hours' sleep before you run into campus for that 12:00 pm submission deadline. You're the kind of person who works best to a deadline, best under pressure – you'll produce a better project report if you stick to the routine.	**A good research project requires a well-structured well-thought-out write-up.** You might choose to write it in a different order than it will be read (introduction last?), but this will require a secondary rewrite or edit from the beginning. Your discussion section should show how your findings relate back to the literature you introduced in the introduction. Do not introduce new material at this point. Ideally edit and proofread it after having put it to one side for a while. Editing may well involve deleting large paragraphs or whole sections that turned out to be irrelevant.

Continued

Continued

How to ruin your research project	How to succeed with your research project
Never mention in a discussion or conclusion the literature you introduced in your introduction – you've covered that stuff already, right? The discussion is the place to write about all that literature you've discovered since you wrote the introduction – it's a great opportunity to mention that stuff which may not be quite relevant but you wanted to show that you've read. Above all, don't go back and edit what you've already written; never delete a paragraph just because you can't remember why you wrote it in the first place – and proofreading is for obsessive compulsives, nuff said! Use the penultimate paragraph to explain to the readers why your project is so poor as they are unlikely to spot this for themselves, and everyone knows that a 'Limitations' section gains you marks. And, finally, everyone knows that the most hard-hitting conclusion a dissertation can make is that 'more research is necessary' – never finish your dissertation without forgetting to make this insightful point.	A good research project requires a balanced, interesting conclusion. The discussions should reflect on the combination of your results and the literature from the introduction. Limitations should be discussed constructively. It can be useful to discuss how future projects might arise from or build on what you've found out here.

Glossary

ANOVA A statistical test used to analyse whether there is a significant difference between results for different groups. Unlike the *t*-test (which can compare only two groups), an ANOVA can compare three or more groups.

average *Average* is a general term for a measure of central tendency. There are three ways to measure the average: mean, median and mode. In common usage, *average* is often understood to refer to the mean.

between group analysis Most variables can be divided into groups, based on some criteria. For example, one may wish to compare the attitudes of people with varying levels of qualification. Forming groups based on each individual's highest qualification may be appropriate.

Bonferroni correction or comparison A Bonferroni correction is used where you want to do several (or many) statistical tests on the same data set. If you just do more and more tests, you are likely to get a significant result by chance (remember that *p* values are probabilities, so chance is an important factor here). The Bonferroni correction adapts this by making it harder to call your result significant (i.e. rather than giving a 0.05 significance level this is corrected to a lower level, e.g. 0.005).

boxplot A powerful visualisation that presents the data from one of more, showing a measure of average, a measure of variance, and minimum and maximum values.

case A single sample (for example a text) or participant (for example a questionnaire respondent) for which data has been collected.

categorical variable Those variables, such as one's occupation or type of vehicle, that do not have numerical values associated with them. This is in contrast to, for example, the number of people in a room or one's height, weight or perhaps blood pressure.

chi square test The chi square test may be used to test the hypothesis of an association between two or more groups, populations or criteria. The chi square test can be conducted either as a 'goodness-of-fit' test, where the data are categorised along one variable, or as a test for the 'contingency table', in which categorisation is across two or more variables. A contingency table was used to compare two groups from separate populations to determine whether there was a significant difference between the expected and observed frequencies. The chi square statistic compares the observed count in each table cell to the count which would be expected under the assumption that there is no association between the row and column classifications.

column chart A chart representing data in vertical columns.

contingency table Categorical data (or different intervals for continuous data) may be displayed in contingency tables. In such a table, frequencies are displayed.

continuous numbers Continuous numbers are those that allow for a continuation of counting on a scale of some kind or as parts of a whole. Continuous numbers include fractions. Unlike natural numbers, whole numbers and integers, fractions are used for measuring, not counting. For example, the American system of measuring ingredients for cooking is based upon a series of cups: 1/4, 1/3, 1/2 and 1. Fractions assign a number as the size of something that is continuous.

Continuous numbers are also represented as *percentages* or other continuous scales such as Celsius and Fahrenheit. Percentages express numbers 'per 100', represented by the % sign. So 1% means 1 per 100.

corpus A large collection of naturally occurring text in electronic format. A corpus is often representative of a specific genre or subject area (for example a collection of interviews or newspaper articles).

correlation An association between two variables. A correlation does not necessarily mean that one causes the other. It often suggests that further analysis could be appropriate.

counting numbers Counting or natural numbers include all of the numbers from 1 to infinity (1, 2, 3, 4, 5, . . .) that we use to count things like apples, boats, pears, people and sheep. The term *infinity* is used here to mean that there is no limit to the magnitude or size of a natural number – the sequence of natural numbers starts at 1 and in theory goes on forever. The set of natural numbers is an ordered sequence of numbers in which each discrete number is one greater than its *predecessor* (the number that appears immediately *before* it in the sequence) and one less than its *successor* (the number that appears immediately *after* it in the sequence). The only exception to this rule is 1, which is the first number in the sequence and has no predecessor.

degrees of freedom   This is a number that represents (but is not equal to) the sample size. It is calculated during statistical testing and is smaller than the sample size. The extent to which it is smaller can depend on the number of parameters the test is examining and whether equal variance can be assumed between groups.

descriptive statistics   Statistics that merely describe but do not suggest any likelihood that the results can be generalised. Measures of the average, the maximum and the minimum are all descriptive, as are visualisations such as pie charts.

distribution   Once certain assumptions are made, one can calculate the probability that a variable has particular values. For example, the distribution of people's heights determines that an individual is much less likely to be between 7 feet and 8 feet tall than they are to be between 5 feet and 6 feet tall. Probability distributions are used to determine expected frequencies.

equality of variance   See 'variance' and 'Levene's test of variance'. When analysing the results of certain statistical tests (for example the *t*-test), you need to be aware of whether the variance among groups can be assumed to be equal or whether there is a significant difference.

expected frequency   A frequency that would occur on the basis of chance alone. For example, if gender was not associated with colour blindness, we would expect a set of values that are similar to what is observed. If the observed values differ significantly from what we expect, then doubt is cast on our assumption of no association.

fractions   Fractions are a type of continuous number and are used for measuring rather than counting. A fraction is a part of a whole. For example, the American system of measuring ingredients for cooking is based upon a series of cups: 1/4, 1/3, 1/2 and 1. In mathematics, four quarters makes up 1, as does two halves. In a fraction such as 1/4, the bottom number, 4, is called the denominator and says how many parts the whole is divided into. The top number, 1, is called the numerator and says how many parts we have.

You can add fractions if the denominator is the same. For example, 1/4 + 1/4 = 2/4. You can reduce or simplify this further by dividing the denominator by the numerator to give 1/2.

frequency   See 'expected frequency' and 'observed frequency'.

frequency distribution   A frequency distribution is a table showing the frequency of various items in samples. For example, it could show the number of occurrences of the perfect and past tenses in texts by different authors.

histogram   A column chart that shows the distribution of data. It can show whether the data has a normal distribution or is skewed.

hypothesis   A hypothesis is a speculative statement about the expected results of a piece of research, based on an educated guess. The aim of the research is then to prove the hypothesis to be (likely to be) true or false. A 'null hypothesis' is the opposite of the hypothesis – the 'status quo'.

integers   An integer is a number that can be negative or positive, but with no fractions. So $-3, -2, -1, 0, 1, 2, 3$ are all integers. In contrast, -1.5 and 3.7 are not.

keyness   In corpus linguistics, measures of keyness are used to identify key words – words whose frequency (or infrequency) in a text or corpus is statistically significant when compared to the standards set by a reference corpus. For example, if you have a collection of British football match reports and use the British National Corpus (a collection of 'general' English) as a reference corpus, you are likely to find 'goal' 'score' and 'ball' to be among the key words.

Kolmogorov-Smirnov test   The Kolmogorov-Smirnov test is used to test normality. If the resulting *significance* figure is greater than 0.05, then the data is normal. For small sample sizes (e.g. less than 50), the Shapiro-Wilk test is more appropriate than the Kolmogorov-Smirnov test.

Levene's test of variance   Variance is a measure of how closely a series of results are clustered around the mean, or how spread out they are from the mean. When one is comparing groups of results, it is important to know whether the variance of each group is roughly equal. Levene's test tells us how significant the difference in variance is.

Likert scale   This is a scale used in questionnaires to measure a positive or negative response to a statement, for example a choice among 7 points on a scale from 'Agree completely' to 'Disagree completely'.

linear   When visualising a relationship between two variables using a scatterplot, if the scattered points follow a straight line, then the relationship is linear. This is important is deciding which measure of correlation to use. See also 'non-linear'.

log likelihood test   In corpus linguistics, the log likelihood test is one way of measuring keyness. See 'keyness' and 'chi square test'.

mean   This involves adding all the values or scores together and dividing by the number of individuals concerned. It provides a measure of the average which is convenient to process. The mean is influenced by very large values. For example, using the mean to calculate average earnings gives a value much higher than the typical income. This is due to the existence of a small number of disproportionately high incomes.

measure of central tendency   A term used to mean 'type of average'. Measures of central tendency are the mean, mode and median.

measure of spread   A measure of spread shows how dispersed or clustered a data set is. Measures of spread include the standard deviation, variance and quartiles.

median   This measure of central tendency (or average) is preferred when dealing with data that has a non-normal distribution. You find it by placing all the data results in order, then picking the number that occurs in the middle.

mode   This measure of central tendency is the value that appears most often in a data set.

natural numbers   See 'counting numbers'.

negative correlation   Where there is a negative correlation between two variables, if one variable increases, the other decreases. If one decreases, the other increases. Correlation is measured on a scale from −1 to +1. The correlation is positive if it is less than 0. The lower the number, the stronger the negative correlation.

nominal numbers   Nominal numbers are numbers used as names – for example the numbers of buses. Because they are merely names, they cannot be used in calculations.

non-linear   When visualising a relationship between two variables using a scatterplot, if the scattered points do not follow a straight line but instead form a curved line, then the relationship is non-linear. This is important because it is deciding which measure of correlation to use. See also 'linear'.

non-parametric tests   These are statistical tests that give reliable results for data sets that do not have a normal distribution and/or do not meet the minimum sample size required by parametric tests. Their calculations use the median, not the mean. They do not have as much statistical power as parametric tests, so if you apply a non-parametric test to data that *could* be analysed with a parametric test, it may miss a significant result.

normalisation   This is *not* to be confused with normality or normal distribution.

Linguistic research is often about making sure that frequency data (how many times a specific linguistic feature occurs) is comparable between texts or corpora. To do this, you would perform statistics on how many times the feature occurs per 100 or 1000 words instead of simply how many times it occurs overall. For example, perhaps you want to compare the frequency of a grammatical feature in ten texts written by one author with its frequency in ten written by another author. The total number of words by author A is 60,000, while the total number by author B is 100,000. To compare the raw frequency of the feature would be misleading because of the difference in the size of the corpora. To account for this, work out the frequency per 1000 words.

observed frequency   Observed frequencies or occurrences represent the data we find in our study. In most studies we assume that there is no link between variables, and we calculate the frequencies which we would expect if no such link existed. If the observed frequencies differ significantly from what we anticipated or expected, then this suggests that a link or association exists. This could form the basis for further study.

one-way ANOVA   A one-way ANOVA allows for the comparison of three or more groups but with just a single variable.

ordinal numbers   Think 'ordinal' = 'order' or 'rank'. Ordinal numbers represent a position or rank in a sequence. For example, the year 2016 is an ordinal number, as is the league position of a football team.

parametric tests   These are statistical tests that give reliable results with data sets that have a normal distribution and/or meet a minimum sample size. Their calculations use the mean as the measure of central tendency. If their conditions are met, they are preferred over non-parametric tests, because they may detect a significant result where a non-parametric test may not find one. The *t*-test and ANOVA are parametric tests.

participants   Often, but not always, the population is made up of people. Any sample will then be made up of individuals. These individuals become the participants in any trial or investigation.

Pearson's correlation coefficient   This statistical test measures the strength and direction of a relationship between two sets of data. It gives a result on a scale from −1 to +1. A score above 0 indicates a positive correlation, and a score below 0 indicates a negative correlation. This figure detects a relationship but cannot detect the cause of that relationship.

percentages   Percentages are continuous numbers that are expressed in relation to 'per 100', represented by the % sign. So 1% means 1 per 100, and 25% means 25 per 100. However, this does not mean you need 100 of something to express a percentage; rather, 100 refers to a total number. For example, if you say that 100% of people questioned said they preferred coffee over tea, then you also need to know how many people were questioned – your *sample*. If the number of people questioned was, say, two, then your finding does not have much validity. If, however, the number questioned was 200 or 2000, then your result will be more reliable.

pie chart   A chart type often over-used by undergraduate students who feel they understand it or who cannot think of another way to calculate numbers as a percentage. They are rarely a good choice of chart type.

population   A population is the entire pool of data items, a complete set of data. A perfect study would measure the whole population, but that does not happen because it is not possible or practical. Instead, a study will take a representative sample from the population, apply statistical tests to the limited data obtained and, from that, try to draw a conclusion that may be true for the whole population.

positive correlation Where there is a positive correlation between two variables, if one variable increases, the other also increases. If one decreases, the other also decreases. Correlation is measured on a scale from −1 to +1. The correlation is positive if it is greater than 0. The higher the number, the stronger the correlation.

post hoc tests A post hoc test is carried out after an ANOVA or other test has shown that there is a significant difference between three or more groups. Typically it will look for differences between all the possible pairs of groups. See Chapter 9 for an example of use of post hoc tests.

power The power of a statistical test refers to its sensitivity, usually in detecting the difference between two groups of data.

probability *Probability* is the measure of the likelihood that an event will occur, that is, how likely it is that something will happen. Probability is quantified as a number between 0 and 1 (where 0 indicates impossibility and 1 indicates certainty). The higher the probability of an event, the more certain we are that the event will occur.

The probability of event A is the number of ways event A can occur divided by the total number of possible outcomes. For example, if a spinner has four equal sectors coloured yellow, blue, green and red, then the probability of landing on any one of the four colours is one in four, so 1/4, or 25%, when one spins the spinner. Another example is that of a die with six sides, where the probability of landing on any one of the numbers 1, 2, 3, 4, 5 and 6 is 1/6.

raw data Raw data is data that has not been altered in any way. For example, if respondents to a questionnaire give their date of birth, that is the raw data. If that data is converted to age, or age category (21–30, 31–40 etc.), then that is no longer raw data.

relative frequency This refers to the normalised score. For example, if a 1000 word text contained 300 pronouns, the relative frequency might be 30 pronouns per 100 words.

research question A research question should be clear and focused and act as the focus of the work undertaken in a research project.

rounding   Rounding is the process of limiting a number to a certain number of decimal places. In quantitative methods, this is particularly apparent when a statistical test gives a figure for significance. In the SPSS software, the rounding is to three decimal places. The figure may appear as 0.000. The significance will never actually be zero, but it may appear to be zero when rounded to three decimal places. Therefore, you should never write in your results '$p = 0.000$'. Instead, you should write '$p < 0.001$'.

sample/sampling   Given that populations are often very large, a sample is drawn from the population. To be meaningful, one aims to select a representative sample, containing all the attributes of the population. If the sample is not representative, bias occurs. This may cause your conclusions to be invalid.

scatterplots   A graphical way to present data points that shows the relationship between two sets of data. An example would be a person's weight plotted against their height.

Shapiro-Wilk test   The Shapiro-Wilk test is used to test normality. If the resulting significance figure is greater than 0.05, then the data is normal. The Shapiro-Wilk test is more appropriate for testing the normality of small sample sizes (e.g. less than 50) than the Kolmogorov-Smirnov test.

significance   When the result of a statistical test is significant, it means that you have, at the very least, reasonable evidence that your observed values were not just due to chance or natural variation alone. For example, if we were testing at 5% significance for an association between colour blindness and gender, then a significant result would mean that such an occurrence would happen by chance alone only on less than 5% of occasions. A 1% significance test, if positive, yields stronger results than a 5% test. We can say that a 1% test is more reliable, although it may take much more work (a bigger sample).

It does not mean that the finding is important or that it has any decision-making utility, but that you are confident that the results are generalisable to the population from which the sample was drawn. A statistically significant difference between two groups could well be very small in real terms. If a result is not statistically significant, we can say that the findings are inconclusive. So statistical significance is concerned with the confidence researchers can have in their findings.

Spearman's correlation coefficient   Like a Pearson's correlation coefficient, this test measures the strength and direction of a relationship between two data sets. It is preferred over a Pearson's test if the data is non-linear.

stacked column chart   A type of column chart that allows comparison of elements within categories. It can present a clearer picture than a grouped column chart where there are more than three or four data sets.

standard deviation   The standard deviation is a statistic that tells you how examples are clustered around the mean in a set of data. When the examples are close together and the bell-shaped curve is steep, the standard deviation is small. When the examples are spread apart and the bell curve is fairly flat, that tells you there is a relatively large standard deviation.

t-test   A *t*-test can identify whether the difference between two data sets is significant. Because the *t*-test is a parametric test, both of the data sets you analyse must fulfil certain criteria for the results to be valid.

There are two main versions of a *t*-test. You use one ('independent samples' or 'two-sample') where you are comparing two data sets that are not linked – for example the weights of women vs the weights of men. You use the other ('paired samples' or 'one-sample') where you are comparing data sets that are linked – for example the weights of the same group of people before and after dieting for a month.

Type 1 and Type 2 statistical errors   Formally, a Type 1 error is the incorrect rejection of a true null hypothesis (a 'false positive'), while a Type 2 error is incorrectly retaining a false null hypothesis. The distinction can also be thought of as the error in asserting a false positive result (e.g. that there is a difference between two groups when in fact there is none) in contrast to that of asserting a false negative (e.g. that there is no difference when in fact a difference might be established by using a statistical test with greater power).

variables   In quantitative methods, a variable is a definition of a data item that you will use for each sample. For example, a survey may use the following variables: name, nationality, age and weight. Variables can be defined as different data types – for example, name and nationality may be defined as 'strings' (that is, names that include letters of the alphabet), while age and weight will be defined as numbers.

variance   Variance is a measure of how closely a series of results are clustered around the mean, or how spread out they are from the mean. When comparing groups of results, it is important to know whether the variance of each group is roughly equal.

whole numbers   If you add the number 0 to the category of natural or counting numbers, you get the category of _whole numbers_ (0, 1, 2, 3, . . .). This is also an example of how a number can be classified as more than one type. For example, the number 2 is both a natural number and a whole number. In fact, all natural numbers are whole numbers, but not all whole numbers are natural numbers. This is because the number 0 is a whole number but not a natural number.

Index